PRAIRIE

PRAIRIE

Cuisine from the Heartland

• • •

STEPHEN LANGLOIS

with Margaret Guthrie

• • •

CB
CONTEMPORARY
BOOKS
CHICAGO

Library of Congress Cataloging-in-Publication Data

Langlois, Stephen.
    Prairie : cuisine from the heartland / Stephen Langlois with
Margaret Guthrie.
      p.   cm.
    Includes index.
    ISBN 0-8092-4114-5 (cloth)
        0-8092-3957-4 (paper)
    1. Cookery, American—Midwestern style.   2. Prairie (Restaurant :
Chicago, Ill.)   I. Guthrie, Margaret E.   II. Title.
TX715.2.M53L36   1990
641.5977—dc20   90-39593
                                                              CIP

Published by Contemporary Books, Inc.
180 North Michigan Avenue, Chicago, Illinois 60601
Manufactured in the United States of America
International Standard Book Number: 0-8092-4114-5 (cloth)
                                      0-8092-3957-4 (paper)

For my father, Jack

CONTENTS

···
ACKNOWLEDGMENTS
···

My sincere thanks go to Rick Cohler, Brian Margulis, and the entire staff of the Chicago Dining Authority, not only for their generosity and loyal support, but also for making us all believe we can do it better. Thanks also to Glenn Gough for his friendship and humorous inspiration; most of all to Jason Tsoris and Paul Harrington and the entire Prairie staff who make me look so good.

This book could not have been written if it weren't for the generous advice and guidance of Dick Whittingham, and for Nancy Crossman, who believed in me and Prairie.

My warmest thanks to my good friend, Margaret Guthrie, who spent countless hours organizing me and my mad ramblings. Her dedication and enthusiasm make this book as much hers as it is mine.

I am most grateful to my family—Lorraine, Scott, Chris, and my grandparents—for all their love and support; to Jacqui, who laughs, cries, and puts up with me every day; and to Pippen and Pumpkin, who eat the leftovers.

Finally, my deepest gratitude to my father, Jack, who inspired me to do this project and who we all love and miss very much.

▪ ▪ ▪
INTRODUCTION
▪ ▪ ▪

Several years ago we decided to create a restaurant that would honor Frank Lloyd Wright's architectural contribution to the world and highlight the best of midwestern food and culinary heritage at the same time. This restaurant would be located in the new Omni Morton Hotel in the architecturally significant Printer's Row area of Chicago.

After graduating from the Culinary Institute of America and cooking for a while in Europe, I found myself engrossed in what seemed the impossible task of creating this regional midwestern menu. At first I was apprehensive about the idea: What was traditional midwestern cooking all about? Was it anything more than just meat and potatoes? How could I create an appealing menu without focusing on today's popular choices of seafood or pasta? Would the finicky Chicago diners really go to a restaurant that devoted itself exclusively to midwestern foodstuffs and had an old-fashioned approach to cooking? With these questions in mind, I rushed off to the local library, interested in finding out just what food from the heartland was and finding out about this guy named Frank Lloyd Wright. I made a couple of startling discoveries: first, that there had been a simple, delicious, and somewhat homey style of cooking practiced in the Midwest for generations; second, that Wright's unique approach to his work provided the perfect way for me to showcase this well-established cuisine.

Now, it's difficult to believe that the work of such an extraordinary architect could have an impact on a young chef's cooking style in today's highly competitive restaurant industry. But Wright's philosophies need not be applied strictly to architecture. His tremendous respect for nature motivated him to combine the building materials found on a given design site, using traditional design techniques. This approach can easily be translated into culinary terms. After all, what is regional cookery but the combination of indigenous ingredients with the traditional cooking techniques of a certain region? Interpreting this approach in greater depth, Wright's architecture can be defined as regional in character, traditional in values, and at the same time uniquely modern. It was with this philosophy in mind that I set out to redefine midwestern cooking.

A year of travel and research throughout the Midwest resulted in the establishment of a network of local suppliers who furnish Prairie with a

virtual cornucopia of high-quality foods on a daily basis. Dried fruits, venison, and morels come from Michigan; wild rice from Minnesota; buffalo, duck, and cheeses from Wisconsin. I was astonished to find out that persimmons are native to Indiana, Ohio is a top producer of tomatoes, and Illinois is the major U.S. producer of pumpkins. It was as interesting meeting the people behind the products: Dean Poulis from Homer's in Evanston, Illinois, who makes ice cream the same way his father did in 1935; or Omar Reese, who drives his station wagon over southwestern Wisconsin's rolling hills, past Frank Lloyd Wright's Taliesin in Spring Green, and brings back some of the best farmstead cheeses I've ever tasted. These cheeses are made by descendants of the original Swiss settlers, using traditional methods that have been handed down from generation to generation. To this day, our never-ending list of suppliers grows, and I look forward to meeting the hundreds more out there.

Searching for the culinary traditions of the region was a vital step in establishing an authentic cuisine. I visited state fairs where I tasted blue-ribbon pies; talked with people about their culinary experiences and memories; ate in restaurants located in rural towns; and even traded recipes with a grandmother or two. I pored over old church and settlement cookbooks looking for useful recipes. I wanted the menu at Prairie to be traditional and wholesome, yet updated and light enough to appeal to today's tastes. I remained adamant about preserving the flavor of each dish, its character and integrity. We kept the best and updated the rest. Some recipes were just too good to change, so I left them exactly as they were.

The final, yet most important, component in redefining the cuisine of the Midwest was the modern approach I had learned so well from the chefs I had worked for. People today are eating foods that are lighter, healthier, and, most of all, fresher than ever before. The end result of any recipe is largely a function of the ingredients used. Therefore, I insist on using only the freshest, highest-quality ingredients available. Fresh herbs are included in many of Prairie's dishes. Seasonal fruits and vegetables are supplied fresh to the restaurant daily. Fish and game come only from reliable suppliers.

The Midwest is probably best known for its simplicity, and that is my "secret ingredient": simple procedures and simple presentations.

This attention to detail, both the historical and the day-to-day, has resulted in a restaurant that was instantly popular with those finicky Chicago diners and almost as instantly recognized for its contribution to the evolution of midwestern cuisine. Because those diners found the food both delicious and different, patrons, local newspapers, and national and international magazines began to ask for recipes. This book was written in answer to those oft-repeated requests.

▪ ▪ ▪
BREAKFAST
▪ ▪ ▪

Breakfast in the Midwest was traditionally as hearty a meal as all the others because it was most often eaten after morning chores. Working before breakfast developed an appetite that did justice to the food on the table.

Prairie's menu reflects this tradition, offering homemade corned beef hash, hashed brown potatoes, and an assortment of pancakes. All of these are wonderful fare for one of today's more popular forms of entertaining: the weekend brunch. The Farmer's Omelet would be fuel enough to get the front lawn raked or the garage cleaned out, or to accomplish any of the other modern chores a family faces. And, fueling up for chores aside, all of these breakfast suggestions are great to linger over with the Sunday paper, accompanied by a good cup of coffee.

CINNAMON RAISIN-NUT OATMEAL

Whoever said that oatmeal doesn't taste good? This recipe combines oatmeal, cinnamon, and vanilla for flavor, honey and sugar for sweetness, and raisins and nuts for texture. It's a healthy, warm start on a cold winter day.

> 1 cup cold water
> ½ cup raisins, loosely packed
> ¾ cup rolled oats
> 1 tablespoon ground cinnamon
> 2 tablespoons dark brown sugar, packed
> 1 tablespoon honey
> ⅛ teaspoon vanilla extract
> ¼ cup toasted, chopped walnuts (see Note)

Combine the water and raisins in a small saucepan and bring to a boil over medium heat. Add the oats, cinnamon, brown sugar, honey, and vanilla.

Reduce the heat to low and cook 10 to 15 minutes, stirring constantly with a wooden spoon, until thick.

Transfer to serving bowls and top with the nuts. Serve immediately.

Note: To toast walnuts, spread them out on a cookie sheet and bake in a preheated 325°F oven for 5 to 8 minutes.

Yield: 2 servings

BAKED APPLE PANCAKE

This also makes a great dessert, served hot with whipped cream or ice cream.

4 Granny Smith apples, peeled,
   cored, and sliced ¼ inch thick
Juice of ½ lemon
¼ teaspoon ground cinnamon
5 tablespoons granulated sugar
5 tablespoons unsalted butter
¼ cup pure maple syrup
4 eggs, beaten
¾ cup all-purpose flour
¾ cup whole milk
Pinch salt

Place the apples in a large bowl and add the lemon juice. Toss lightly. Combine the cinnamon and sugar and sprinkle over the apples. Toss well.

In a medium-sized sauté pan, melt 3 tablespoons of the butter. Add the apple mixture and sauté over medium heat for 8 to 10 minutes. Add the maple syrup and continue cooking until the apples are soft, but not mushy, and the syrup has reduced to a thick glaze—about 12 to 15 minutes. Set aside.

Preheat the oven to 425°F. In a bowl combine the eggs, flour, milk, and salt. Blend until smooth.

In a medium-sized, ovenproof sauté pan, heat the remaining 2 tablespoons of butter. Add the reserved apple mixture and spread evenly over the bottom of the pan. Cook over medium heat for 2 to 3 minutes, until hot. Pour the batter over the apples and, without stirring or mixing, cook over medium heat for another 2 to 3 minutes. Place the whole pan in the preheated oven and cook for about 15 minutes, until puffy and golden brown. Cut into wedges and serve immediately.

Yield: 1 large or 2 small pancakes (1 to 2 servings)

DUTCH BABIES

These thin, flat pancakes are rumored to have originated with the Mennonites of Indiana and Ohio.

6 eggs, beaten
1 cup whole milk
1 cup all-purpose flour
¼ teaspoon salt
1 tablespoon unsalted butter
4 lemon wedges
Powdered sugar as needed

Preheat the oven to 425°F. In a bowl combine the eggs, milk, flour, and salt. Mix well until smooth.

To make one Dutch Baby, heat the butter in an 8-inch ovenproof skillet and pour in ½ cup batter. Tilt the pan to make a thin, even coating of batter on the bottom and up the sides of the pan.

Place the whole pan in the preheated oven and bake for 10 to 12 minutes, until the edges are just barely crispy. Remove the pan from the oven and serve immediately. Sprinkle with the powdered sugar and serve with lemon wedges. Dutch Babies go great with good-quality (homemade) jam or preserves.

Yield: 4 Dutch Babies (4 servings)

STATE FAIR FUNNEL CAKES

At state fairs and carnivals all over the Midwest there are little trailers that sell funnel cakes and curly fries. Like hot dogs at the ball park, they always seem to taste better there.

Oil for deep-frying
2 tablespoons sour cream
2 tablespoons unsalted butter,
 softened
2 eggs, beaten
¼ cup light brown sugar, packed
3½ cups all-purpose flour
2 tablespoons baking powder
1 cup heavy cream
⅓ cup honey
Powdered sugar
Ground cinnamon

Preheat a deep fryer to 350°F. In the bowl of an electric mixer fitted with a whip, combine the sour cream, butter, eggs, and brown sugar. Whip on high speed for about 5 minutes, until smooth and frothy.

Add the flour, baking powder, and cream and whip on low speed just until the batter comes together. Don't worry about lumps; they will disappear during cooking.

Let the batter rest, refrigerated, for at least 15 minutes before using.

Holding a clean funnel about 1 inch above the hot fat, carefully pour the batter through the funnel, moving it in a circular pattern; use 4 to 5 tablespoons for each cake. Cook about 2 to 3 minutes on each side, until puffed and golden brown.

Remove with a slotted spoon and drain well on paper towels. Serve immediately with honey on the side and dust generously with the powdered sugar and cinnamon.

Yield: 6 cakes (6 servings)

STUFFED FRENCH TOAST

For a little variety replace the strawberry preserves with another flavor, or better yet, use the top-quality preserves and marmalades called Spoon Fruits from American Spoon Foods (see Sources for Midwest Specialties).

16 slices good white bread
½ cup good strawberry preserves
6 eggs, beaten
¼ cup whole milk
4 tablespoons (½ stick) unsalted
   butter
Powdered sugar
Ground cinnamon
Butter
Maple syrup

Lay out eight slices of the bread and spread with the strawberry preserves. Place the other eight slices of bread on top to make eight strawberry-preserve sandwiches. Set aside.

In a large bowl combine the eggs and milk. Whisk well, using a wire whisk, until smooth. Heat the butter in a large sauté pan or cast-iron skillet over medium heat.

Dip the sandwiches in the egg mixture and carefully place them in the pan. Sauté until well browned on both sides. Drain well on paper towels and transfer to a serving platter. Dust with powdered sugar and cinnamon and serve topped with butter and maple syrup.

Yield: 4 servings

YEAST WAFFLES WITH STEWED BLUEBERRIES

This dish should be started a day in advance. Try replacing the blueberries with other fresh berries such as blackberries, strawberries, or raspberries.

STEWED BLUEBERRIES
1 quart ripe blueberries
½ cup granulated sugar
Juice of ½ lemon
½ teaspoon ground cinnamon
⅛ teaspoon ground nutmeg
2 tablespoons cornstarch

WAFFLES
1 tablespoon dry yeast
¼ cup warm water
Pinch granulated sugar
2 cups all-purpose flour
¼ cup granulated sugar
½ teaspoon salt
½ teaspoon baking soda
1¼ cups whole milk
8 tablespoons (1 stick) unsalted
   butter, melted and cooled
3 eggs, beaten

Pick over the berries and rinse them under cold water, discarding all stems. Drain well.

Combine the blueberries, sugar, lemon juice, cinnamon, nutmeg, and cornstarch in a medium-sized saucepan. Place the pan over medium heat and cook, stirring constantly, until the berries have broken and the syrup is thick, approximately 15 to 20 minutes.

Transfer the berries to a nonreactive container and refrigerate overnight before using.

Prepare the waffles by combining the yeast, water, and pinch of sugar in the bowl of an electric mixer fitted with a paddle. Stir well to dissolve, and let the mixture rest for 10 to 15 minutes. In the meantime, sift together the flour, ¼ cup sugar, salt, and baking soda. Set aside.

Add the milk, butter, and eggs to the yeast mixture and mix well to combine. Add the reserved flour mixture and mix on low speed just until all the ingredients have combined and a smooth batter is formed.

Cover the batter tightly and put it in a warm place for approximately 2 hours. Preheat a waffle iron, and when hot enough, gently ladle the amount specified in the manufacturer's directions. Cook, again following the manufacturer's instructions. Serve hot, topped with the stewed blueberries.

Yield: Approximately 6 waffles (6 servings)

OLD-FASHIONED CORNED BEEF HASH

All really good restaurants in the Midwest that prepare breakfast serve a really good homemade corned beef hash. This particular version is a perfect dish for a Sunday brunch buffet, accompanied by scrambled eggs or served plain with melted cheddar cheese. Be sure to serve this hot and well browned and crispy on the outside.

1 cup cooked, finely chopped
   corned beef
2 cups cooked, coarsely chopped
   potatoes
½ tablespoon Worcestershire sauce
¼ cup whole milk
¼ cup Basic Chicken Stock (see
   Index)
Salt to taste
Freshly ground black pepper to
   taste
¼ cup bacon fat or vegetable oil

In a large bowl combine the corned beef, potatoes, Worcestershire sauce, milk, and chicken stock. Mix well to bind. Season to taste with salt and freshly ground black pepper.

Heat a large cast-iron skillet over medium heat until very hot, about 10 to 12 minutes. Add the bacon fat or oil. Divide the hash evenly into four portions. Add each batch to the pan and flatten with the bottom of a spatula. Reduce the heat to low and and cook 8 to 10 minutes, until brown and crispy on each side. Serve immediately.

Yield: 4 servings

FARMER'S OMELET

Try substituting other vegetables for those listed in this recipe, or better yet, use leftover vegetables here. I prefer to use a nice aged sharp cheddar cheese in this omelet, but you can use your own favorite cheese. Make the Crispy Hash Browns as an accompaniment and serve with catsup to be authentically midwestern.

2 eggs, beaten
2 tablespoons whole milk
2 tablespoons unsalted butter
2 tablespoons finely chopped
 green bell pepper
2 tablespoons finely chopped
 tomato
2 tablespoons finely diced
 zucchini
3 mushrooms, washed and sliced
 fine
4 broccoli florets, cut into very
 small pieces
¼ cup shredded sharp cheddar
 cheese
Salt to taste
Freshly ground black pepper to
 taste

Combine the eggs and milk. Whisk well and set aside. Heat the butter in a medium-sized nonstick pan. Add the vegetables and cook over high heat for 5 minutes.

Preheat the broiler.

Add the egg mixture and with a wooden spoon stir constantly in a circular motion while moving the pan back and forth. Reduce the heat to medium and cook until the eggs are nearly set.

Sprinkle the cheese evenly on top of the omelet. Place the pan under the broiler until the cheese melts. Fold the omelet in thirds, folding the edges toward the middle. Serve seam side down on the plate. Season to taste with salt and pepper.

Yield: 1 omelet

PRAIRIE-STYLE EGGS BENEDICT

This is the perfect dish to serve for Sunday brunch. I was inspired to develop it because of the overwhelming demand at Prairie for the traditional eggs Benedict. In order to make it more midwestern I combined Crispy Hash Browns, Old-Fashioned Corned Beef Hash, and a silky Cheddar Cheese Hollandaise. It has been our hottest-selling breakfast item ever since it hit the menu.

>1 recipe Crispy Hash Browns (see
>   Index)
>1 recipe Old-Fashioned Corned
>   Beef Hash (see Index)
>1 tablespoon white vinegar
>8 eggs
>1 recipe Cheddar Cheese
>   Hollandaise (recipe follows)
>1 scallion, chopped fine

Arrange the hash browns on a serving platter and top with the corned beef hash. Set aside and keep hot.

Fill a medium-sized saucepan two-thirds full with water and add the vinegar. Bring the water to a simmer and crack the eggs into the water. Cook the eggs in the simmering water for approximately 4 minutes, or until the whites are firm but the yolks are still runny.

Using a slotted spoon, very carefully remove the eggs one by one, making sure not to break the yolks. Drain well. Place the eggs on top of the corned beef hash (2 per serving). Top with the hollandaise and sprinkle with the chopped scallion. Serve immediately.

Yield: 4 servings

CHEDDAR CHEESE HOLLANDAISE

1½ cups (3 sticks) unsalted butter, melted
4 egg yolks
2 eggs
4 tablespoons warm water
4 tablespoons lemon juice
2 teaspoons cider vinegar
½ teaspoon granulated sugar
¼ teaspoon cayenne pepper
¼ teaspoon Tabasco
½ teaspoon Worcestershire sauce
2 tablespoons heavy cream
¼ cup grated sharp cheddar cheese

Allow the melted butter to rest for 8 to 10 minutes until the solids are resting on the bottom of the pan. Carefully separate the clarified butter from the solids, using a ladle and a double thickness of cheesecloth. Discard the solids. Set aside the clarified butter and keep it warm.

In a nonreactive bowl, combine the egg yolks, eggs, water, lemon juice, vinegar, sugar, cayenne pepper, Tabasco, and Worcestershire sauce. Place the bowl on top of a pan of simmering water and whisk vigorously until the mixture forms a thick custard that holds very soft peaks.

Remove from the heat and, while whisking constantly, add the clarified butter, drop by drop, until the mixture starts to thicken. During this process be careful not to overheat the mixture, which causes it to get too thick or shiny. If it does overheat, add a little water or lemon juice to thin it out. Continue to whisk until all the butter has been incorporated.

In the top of a double boiler combine the cream and the cheddar cheese and heat until the cheese has melted. Add the melted cheese to the hollandaise sauce and whisk well to combine. Keep the sauce warm and serve immediately.

Yield: 2 cups sauce

CRISPY HASH BROWNS

If you have any leftover baked or boiled potatoes, use them here to cut down on preparation time. Be sure to serve these immediately so that they stay crispy on the outside and moist on the inside.

2 pounds russet potatoes
1 onion, peeled, and chopped fine
4 tablespoons bacon fat or
    vegetable oil
Salt to taste
Freshly ground black pepper to
    taste

Place the potatoes in a large saucepan and cover with cold water. Place the pan on high heat and bring the water to a full, rolling boil. Boil the potatoes for 15 minutes.

Remove the potatoes from the water and run them under cold water. When the potatoes are cool enough to handle, gently peel off their skins. Discard the skins.

Coarsely grate the potatoes on a cheese grater. Add the chopped onion and toss well to mix. Heat a large cast-iron skillet over medium heat for 10 to 12 minutes, until very hot. Add the bacon fat or oil. Divide the potatoes evenly into four batches. Add each batch of potatoes separately and flatten out with the back of a spatula.

Reduce the heat to medium and cook until golden brown, about 5 minutes on each side. Remove and drain well on paper towels. Season well with salt and pepper. Serve immediately.

Yield: 4 servings

BREADS AND MUFFINS

Breads are one of the mainstays of many cuisines, and this is certainly the case in the Midwest. The Midwest has the additional advantage of being a region amenable to the growing of grains, which is why it's called "the nation's breadbasket." It's also an area where many other ingredients that are wonderful additions to basic bread recipes grow well or are produced—ingredients like apple cider, honey, butternut squash, aged cheddar cheese, and maple syrup, all of which turn what might be ordinary bread into something special.

The farming tradition of this region led to hearty meals and equally hearty appetites. Breads, biscuits, muffins, and rolls regularly came to the table to accompany the meats and vegetables raised on the property. Prairie's interpretations of some of these old recipes will give you a whole new appreciation of bread and its variations.

WISCONSIN CHEDDAR CHEESE AND CHIVE DROP BISCUITS

These ancestors of baking-soda biscuits were popular back in the days of the pioneers when rations were limited and cooking procedures necessarily simplified. They are light, flavorful, and, most of all, easy to make. Serve them with corn chowder or as an accompaniment to a salad.

$1\frac{2}{3}$ cups all-purpose flour
2 teaspoons baking powder
$\frac{1}{2}$ teaspoon baking soda
$\frac{1}{4}$ teaspoon salt
$\frac{2}{3}$ stick unsalted butter, cut into
    small (1 inch) cubes
$\frac{3}{4}$ cup grated sharp cheddar cheese
$1\frac{1}{2}$ tablespoons chopped fresh
    chives
$\frac{3}{4}$ cup buttermilk

Preheat the oven to 400°F. Lightly grease a cookie sheet and set it aside.

Sift together the flour, baking powder, baking soda, and salt into a large bowl. Add the butter and, using a pastry blender or fork, cut the butter into the dry ingredients until the mixture resembles coarse meal.

Add the cheddar cheese and the chopped chives and toss lightly to combine.

Add the buttermilk and stir vigorously with a wooden spoon until the mixture just comes together. Do not overmix.

Spoon the batter onto the reserved, greased cookie sheet in 2- to 3-tablespoon drops, placed $1\frac{1}{2}$ to 2 inches apart. Bake in the preheated oven for 12 to 14 minutes or until golden brown. Serve immediately.

Yield: 12 biscuits

BUCKWHEAT HONEY BREAD

This is a great bread to use for toast or ham sandwiches. It is an heirloom recipe that was given to me by a woman I met at the Iowa State Fair a few years ago. She used ground black walnuts her daughter had sent her from Missouri, but it tastes just as good with ground pecans, walnuts, or hazelnuts. If you really feel adventurous, try a combination of a few different nuts.

2 pounds bread flour
½ teaspoon salt
2½ tablespoons dry yeast
2 cups buckwheat flour
1½ cups water
¾ cup honey
¾ pound (3 sticks) unsalted
    margarine, melted
1½ cups small-curd cottage cheese
3 eggs, beaten
1½ cups whole-wheat flour
¾ cup rolled oats
1 cup ground nuts

In the bowl of an electric mixer or food processor, combine the bread flour, salt, yeast, and buckwheat flour. Blend well. Set aside. In a saucepan heat the water, honey, margarine, and cottage cheese until the mixture is warm (110 to 120°F).

Add the warm honey mixture to the reserved flour mixture and add the eggs. Blend at low speed until the mixture is well moistened. Add the whole-wheat flour, oats, and nuts to form a soft dough. Increase the speed to medium and blend for 3 minutes.

Remove the dough to a floured surface and knead for 5 minutes, until the dough is smooth and elastic. Place in a well-greased bowl, turn to coat the surface of the dough, and cover tightly with plastic wrap.

Let the dough rise in a warm, draft-free place until it doubles in bulk (about 1 hour). Preheat the oven to 325°F. Generously butter two 9″ × 5″ loaf pans.

Remove the dough from the bowl and punch it down. Knead again for 2 to 3 minutes. Cover with a clean, dry towel and let rest for 15 minutes. Split the dough in half; roll each half out in a rectangle the length of the pan. Roll the rectangles up into loaf shapes, pinching the ends. Place in the buttered tins, cover with the clean, dry towel, and let rise until double in volume, about 20 minutes. Bake in the preheated oven for about 1 hour and 15 minutes, or until done. (Rap the bread with your knuckles; if the bread is done, it will sound hollow.)

Yield: 2 medium-sized loaves

CIDER-SQUASH BREAD

I always make this bread in the fall when apples and squashes are in abundance. It has a slightly sweet flavor, offset by a little tanginess from the cheddar cheese. Serve it warm with Apple Butter (see Index) or, better yet, use it for French toast.

2½ tablespoons dry yeast
⅔ cup granulated sugar
¾ cup lukewarm apple cider (110 to 120°F)
1 cup (2 sticks) unsalted butter, melted
2 tablespoons salt
8 eggs, beaten
7 cups bread flour
1½ cups all-purpose flour
1¼ cups cooked and pureed butternut squash (see Note)
¼ cup wheat germ
⅔ cup grated cheddar cheese

Combine the yeast with 1 tablespoon of the sugar in the bowl of an electric mixer. Add the apple cider and mix well. Let the yeast proof for 5 minutes.

Add the remaining sugar, butter, salt, and eggs to the yeast mixture and blend well. Remove the beaters from the mixer and put on the dough hook(s). Add the flours, squash, wheat germ, and cheese and mix for 5 minutes on medium speed. The dough should be sticky.

Remove the dough to a floured surface and knead for 5 minutes until it is smooth and elastic. Place the dough in a well-greased bowl, turn to coat the dough thoroughly, and cover tightly with plastic wrap. Put the bowl in a warm, draft-free place and allow the dough to rise until double in bulk, about 1 hour.

Preheat the oven to 300°F. Generously butter two 9″ × 5″ loaf pans. Divide the dough in half, and roll out each half into a rectangle. Remove dough to floured surface and punch it down. Knead again for 2 minutes. Cover with a clean, dry towel and let rest for 15 minutes. Roll up each

rectangle along the long side to form a loaf. Pinch the ends and place the loaves in the pans. Cover the loaves with a clean, dry towel and allow to rise in a warm place until double in volume, about 20 to 30 minutes. Bake in the preheated oven for about an hour or until the bread sounds hollow when rapped with a knuckle.

Note: To make 1¼ cups pureed butternut squash begin with 2 pounds of squash. Preheat the oven to 350°F. Cut the squash in half and remove the seeds. Place on small cookie sheet and cover with aluminum foil. Bake on the center rack of the preheated oven for 25 to 30 minutes until very soft (test by piercing with a fork). Remove from the oven and, when the squash is cool enough to handle, scoop the flesh off the rind using a spoon. Place in a food processor fitted with a steel blade and puree until smooth and velvety.

Yield: 2 medium-sized loaves

FARMHOUSE POTATO BREAD

What would we do here in the heartland without our potatoes? We love 'em! This is truly a unique bread that probably was brought to the Midwest by the European immigrants who settled here long ago. The glaze is intended to make the crust shiny and crispy and not to sweeten it. This bread is a little dense and resembles a good sourdough or Italian bread.

> 3 cups whole milk
> 1½ cups (3 sticks) unsalted butter
> 3 cups warm Creamy Mashed
>   Potatoes (see Index)
> 1½ cups honey
> 2½ tablespoons dry yeast
> 1½ cups lukewarm (110 to 120°F)
>   potato water (same water
>   potatoes were cooked in)
> 1 tablespoon granulated sugar
> 1 tablespoon ground ginger
> 6 eggs, beaten
> 2 tablespoons salt
> 14 cups bread flour
> 7 cups all-purpose flour
>
> GLAZE
> ¼ cup honey
> 1½ cups heavy cream

Bring the milk to a boil in a medium-sized saucepan and add the butter, mashed potatoes, and honey. Mix well and set aside to cool. In the bowl of an electric mixer fitted with a paddle, dissolve the yeast in the water and add the sugar. Let the yeast proof for 5 minutes.

Add the reserved lukewarm potato mixture to the yeast mixture along with the ginger, eggs, and salt. Beat well. Add 1 cup of the bread flour and 1 cup of the all-purpose flour and mix on medium speed for 2 to 3 minutes, scraping down the sides of the bowl when necessary.

Put the dough hook on the electric mixer. Gradually add the rest of the bread flour and the all-purpose flour. Mix well for about 5 minutes. The dough should be soft and sticky. Preheat the oven to 325°F. Generously butter two 9″ × 5″ loaf pans.

Remove the dough to a floured surface and knead for 5 minutes, until it is smooth and elastic. Place the dough in a well-greased bowl and turn to coat the dough on all sides. Cover tightly with plastic wrap and allow to rise in a warm, draft-free place for about an hour, or until double in volume.

Transfer the dough from the bowl back to the floured surface and punch it down. Knead again for 5 minutes. Let the dough rest for 15 minutes, covered with a clean towel. Divide the dough evenly in half and roll each half into a rectangle. Roll up the rectangles the long way, pinch the ends to seal, and put in the loaf pans.

Allow to rise in a warm place until double in volume, about 25 minutes. Combine the honey and the cream for the glaze, mixing well. Bake the bread in the preheated oven for about an hour, or until it sounds hollow when rapped with a knuckle. Remove and glaze while still hot.

Yield: 4 medium-sized loaves

CINNAMON ROLLS

Cinnamon rolls are as commonplace in the Midwest as lobsters are in New England. Here they make 'em big—about the size of a softball!

DOUGH
2 tablespoons dry yeast
¼ cup lukewarm water (110 to 120°F)
1 tablespoon granulated sugar
2 eggs, beaten
1 cup whole milk
2 tablespoons unsalted butter, melted
1 teaspoon salt
3½ cups all-purpose flour
1 cup (2 sticks) unsalted butter, melted
1 cup granulated sugar
¼ cup ground cinnamon

TOPPING
1½ cups dark brown sugar, packed
½ cup (1 stick) unsalted butter, melted
½ cup heavy cream

ICING
1 cup powdered sugar
2 tablespoons whole milk
1 tablespoon unsalted butter, softened
½ teaspoon vanilla extract

Preheat the oven to 350°F. Generously grease a small sheet pan with shallow sides.

In the bowl of an electric mixer fitted with a whip, combine the yeast and water. Stir well to dissolve. Sprinkle the tablespoon of sugar over the top and let the mixture stand for 15 minutes.

Add the eggs, milk, and the 2 tablespoons melted butter. Whip on medium speed until well blended.

Sift together the salt and flour and add to the yeast mixture. Remove the whip from the mixer and attach a dough hook. Beat on medium speed until the mixture comes together to form a smooth dough.

Remove to a well-floured board and knead the dough for 5 minutes, until smooth and elastic. Place the dough in a well-greased bowl, turn to coat the dough, and cover with a clean, damp towel or with plastic wrap. Place in a warm, draft-free area and let the dough rise for approximately 30 minutes or until it has doubled in bulk.

In the meantime, prepare the topping. Combine the brown sugar, melted butter, and cream in a medium saucepan. Cook over medium heat, stirring constantly, to dissolve the sugar. Remove from the heat and pour into the greased sheet pan. Set aside.

Put the dough back on the floured board and punch down. Let rest for 15 minutes covered with a clean, dry towel. Roll the dough out into an even rectangle about ¼ inch thick.

Brush the dough generously with the cup of melted butter and sprinkle the whole rectangle evenly with the cup of sugar and the cinnamon. Starting at the top edge of the dough, carefully and tightly roll it down to the bottom edge, creating a tight roll.

Using a sharp knife, cut the dough into 12 equal rolls. Place the rolls on the reserved sheet pan in the topping. Cover lightly with a clean, damp towel and put back in a warm, draft-free place for about 40 minutes, or until the rolls have doubled in volume. Bake in the preheated oven for approximately 30 minutes, or until golden brown and firm to the touch.

Remove the pan from the oven and let the rolls cool for 15 minutes. Prepare the icing by combining the sugar, milk, butter, and vanilla in a bowl and whisking until smooth. Invert the cinnamon rolls onto a serving platter and drizzle with the icing. Serve warm.

Yield: 12 rolls

RHUBARB-RAISIN-NUT ROLLS

In Michigan, around the end of May, it has been said that rhubarb grows like weeds. I love the flavor of rhubarb and try to use it in season as much as possible. For this recipe, however, you may substitute frozen rhubarb by first sautéing it in a little butter and using the juices that accumulate in conjunction with the orange juice.

1 cup washed and finely chopped fresh rhubarb
½ cup granulated sugar
¼ cup orange juice
¾ cup raisins
1 tablespoon dry yeast
⅓ cup lukewarm water (110 to 120°F)
2 tablespoons granulated sugar
2 cups all-purpose flour
2 cups bread flour
1 teaspoon salt
½ teaspoon baking soda
½ tablespoon ground cinnamon
¼ teaspoon ground nutmeg
½ teaspoon ground ginger
2 eggs, beaten
½ cup buttermilk
2 tablespoons unsalted butter, melted
½ cup toasted, chopped walnuts (see Note)

GLAZE
¼ cup honey
4 tablespoons (½ stick) unsalted butter
2 tablespoons half-and-half

Preheat the oven to 350°F. Grease a cookie sheet and set aside.

In a medium saucepan, combine the rhubarb, sugar, and orange juice. Cook over medium heat for 20 minutes, then remove from the heat. Add the raisins and let the mixture cool to room temperature.

In the bowl of an electric mixer fitted with a paddle, dissolve the yeast in the warm water and sprinkle the sugar over the top. Let stand for 10 to 15 minutes.

Sift together the flours, salt, baking soda, cinnamon, nutmeg, and ginger. Set aside.

Combine the eggs, buttermilk, and melted butter with the yeast mixture and mix well on medium speed until smooth. Remove the paddle from the mixer and replace it with the dough hook. Add the rhubarb mixture, sifted dry ingredients, and the chopped nuts. Mix well on low speed, just until the ingredients come together.

Remove the dough to a floured board and knead for approximately 5 minutes, until smooth and elastic. Place the dough in a well-greased bowl and turn to coat on all sides. Cover with a clean, damp cloth or with plastic wrap. Set in a warm, draft-free place and let rise for 1 hour or until double in bulk.

Remove the dough to the floured board and punch down. Let stand for 15 minutes. Form into 2-inch rolls and place them on the reserved, greased cookie sheet, approximately 2 inches apart. Cover with a clean, damp cloth and let rise until double in bulk, about 30 minutes.

Prepare the glaze by combining the honey, butter, and half-and-half in a small saucepan. Cook over low heat until the butter has melted and all the ingredients are combined. Set aside and keep warm. Stir well before using.

Bake the rolls on the center rack of the preheated oven for 30 to 35 minutes, until golden brown and firm to the touch. Remove from the oven and glaze immediately. Serve warm with Apple Butter (see Index).

Note: To toast walnuts, spread them out on a cookie sheet and bake in a preheated 325°F oven for 5 to 8 minutes.

Yield: Approximately 15 rolls

APPLE-WALNUT MUFFINS

I would go so far as to say that the Midwest is the undisputed home of the world's best muffin chefs. They make them as big as baseballs yet as light as soufflés here and serve them as a meal for breakfast, or as bread with dinner. This is one of my personal favorites. If you like them sweet, use red Delicious apples; if you like them less sweet, use Granny Smiths; and for a really intense apple flavor, serve them with Apple Butter (see Index).

2½ cups all-purpose flour
1 tablespoon baking powder
1 teaspoon baking soda
½ teaspoon ground nutmeg
½ tablespoon ground cinnamon
½ teaspoon salt
½ cup light brown sugar, packed
2 eggs, beaten
¾ cup buttermilk
⅓ cup unsalted butter, melted
2 cups grated apple
½ cup toasted, chopped walnuts (see Note)

Preheat the oven to 400°F. Grease 12 muffin cups and set aside.

Sift together the flour, baking powder, baking soda, nutmeg, cinnamon, and salt. Set aside.

In the bowl of an electric mixer fitted with a paddle, combine the brown sugar, eggs, buttermilk, and melted butter. Beat on medium speed until the mixture is smooth.

Add the reserved dry ingredients and beat on low speed just until the ingredients are combined. Don't worry about lumps; they will disappear during baking. Gently fold in the grated apple and the walnuts. Spoon into the prepared muffin tins.

Place on the center rack of the preheated oven and bake for 25 minutes, until golden brown and firm to the touch. Serve hot.

Note: To toast walnuts, spread them out on a cookie sheet and bake in a preheated 325°F oven for 5 to 8 minutes.

Yield: 12 muffins

BLUEBERRY MUFFINS

No midwestern cookbook would be complete without a recipe for the classic blueberry muffin. Always use fresh blueberries when they are available, and if they are not, try substituting other fresh berries, such as blackberries or raspberries. Frozen berries can be used, but they tend to make these muffins soggy. In any case, serve them piping hot, slapped with a little soft butter.

> 2½ cups all-purpose flour
> ½ cup granulated sugar
> 2 tablespoons baking powder
> ½ teaspoon baking soda
> ½ teaspoon salt
> 1 cup fresh blueberries
> 2 eggs, beaten
> 1 cup whole milk
> 4 tablespoons (½ stick) unsalted
>   butter, melted

Preheat the oven to 400°F. Generously grease 12 muffin cups and set aside.

Sift together the flour, sugar, baking powder, baking soda, and salt. Set aside. Pick over and wash the blueberries; drain them well and set aside.

In the bowl of an electric mixer fitted with a paddle, combine the eggs, milk, and butter. Mix well on medium speed to combine the ingredients.

Add the reserved dry ingredients and mix on slow speed just until the ingredients come together. Don't worry about lumps; they will disappear during baking.

Gently toss the blueberries in a little extra flour and carefully fold them into the muffin mixture using a rubber spatula.

Spoon the batter into the prepared muffin cups. Bake on the center rack of the preheated oven for approximately 25 minutes, until they are golden brown and firm to the touch. Serve hot.

Yield: 12 muffins

CARROT-RAISIN-BRAN MUFFINS

These muffins remind me of little carrot cakes. For a real treat, try frosting them with Cream-Cheese Frosting (see Index) and serving them to the kids as Carrot-Raisin-Bran Cupcakes.

2 cups all-purpose flour
1 tablespoon baking powder
¼ teaspoon salt
½ teaspoon ground nutmeg
½ teaspoon ground allspice
½ tablespoon ground cinnamon
2½ cups All Bran flakes
1 cup whole milk
½ cup light brown sugar, packed
4 tablespoons (½ stick) unsalted
    butter, melted
2 eggs, beaten
1 tablespoon molasses
1½ cups grated and peeled carrot
½ cup raisins

Preheat the oven to 400°F. Generously grease 12 muffin cups. Set aside.
Sift together the flour, baking powder, salt, and spices. Set aside.
In the bowl of an electric mixer, combine the bran flakes and the milk. Let stand for 10 to 15 minutes, until the bran flakes have become soggy. Add the brown sugar, melted butter, eggs, and molasses. Beat on low speed just until all the ingredients are combined. Add the reserved dry ingredients and blend on low speed, again just until the ingredients come together. Don't worry about lumps; they will disappear during baking.
Using a rubber spatula, gently fold in the grated carrot and raisins. Spoon into the prepared muffin tins and bake on the center rack of the preheated oven for 25 to 30 minutes, until golden brown and firm to the touch. Serve hot.

Yield: 12 muffins

SOUPS AND STARTERS

Soup is a universal dish; every cuisine worldwide has at least one that's nationally, if not internationally, recognized. It's usually an easy dish to prepare and sustaining to eat. Soups can range from near-stews in contents and texture to the most ephemeral broths seasoned with lightly smoked meats or fresh herbs. The Midwest has plenty to offer in the realm of soup, and Prairie serves some wonderful variations on ancient themes: Corn Chowder with Fresh Herbs and Country-Smoked Ham or a simple Cream of Asparagus.

Appetizers, or starters, as they are called in the Midwest, are dishes designed to awaken the appetite. They're generally considered a prelude to the wonderful things to come. Some restaurants offer such wonderful starters that a meal can easily be made from two or three of them. Prairie is certainly such a restaurant, offering as it does such tempters as Brandied Game Loaf, Regional Mushroom Sauté in an Onion-Dill Biscuit with Morel Puree, and Warm Apple and Sage Sausage Turnovers with a Cider-Cranberry Glaze.

BASIC CHICKEN STOCK

A pot of stock simmering on the back of the stove is the secret ingredient or key to making a wealth of delicious, flavorful midwestern dishes. Follow the directions carefully and remember to let the stock simmer slowly while skimming off any foam that appears on the surface.

> 5 pounds chicken carcasses
> 1 medium carrot
> 2 medium ribs celery, washed
> 1 large onion, peeled
> 1 bay leaf
> 2 parsley stems
> 2 sprigs fresh tarragon
> 2 sprigs fresh thyme
> ¼ teaspoon whole black
>   peppercorns
> 6 cups cold water

Using a cleaver or chef's knife, cut up the carcasses into 1- to 2-inch chunks. Peel and slice the carrot into 1-inch chunks, cut the celery into 1-inch chunks, and cut the onion in sixths.

Place the carcass chunks in a large stockpot and add all the other ingredients. Mix well to distribute the ingredients evenly. Place the stockpot on high heat and bring to a full, rolling boil.

Reduce the heat and simmer, uncovered, for 6 to 8 hours, skimming the fat and foam as it appears on the surface of the stock.

Remove the stock from the fire and strain carefully through a double layer of cheesecloth into a heatproof container. Place the container in a sink filled with ice water. Stir occasionally until the stock reaches room temperature. If using in the next few days, simply refrigerate. If not, pour into small freezer containers and freeze until needed.

Yield: 1 quart

REDUCED VEAL STOCK

Stocks and broths are very important components in modern cooking. People often ask how I make my sauces taste so good, and I reply that it's all in the stock. When building a house, it is vital to build a good foundation. When making a soup or a sauce, it is also vital to start with a good foundation—the stock. Although the cooking time is quite lengthy, stocks require very little effort by the cook once they are simmering. I know of no substitute for a well-made stock, and I think it's well worth the effort to make one so that you can start with that good foundation.

12 pounds veal bones (preferably
   neck bones)
2 medium onions, skin on, sliced
   thin
3 medium carrots, peeled and
   sliced 1 inch thick
3 medium ribs celery, washed and
   sliced 1 inch thick
½ cup tomato paste
2 parsley stems
2 sprigs fresh thyme
3 sprigs fresh tarragon
2 tablespoons whole black
   peppercorns
1 gallon cold water

Preheat the oven to 375°F. Place the veal bones in a large roasting pan on the middle shelf of the preheated oven. Roast for 1 hour, turning the bones occasionally.

Add the onions, carrots, celery, and tomato paste and cook for 1½ to 2 hours longer, or until both the bones and the vegetables are well browned.

Transfer the bones and the vegetables to a large stockpot and pour off all excess fat from the roasting pan. Return the pan to the top of the stove, add about 1 quart of the water, and bring to a boil while scraping the bottom of the pan to loosen the drippings. Pour this liquid over the bones in the stockpot.

Add the remaining ingredients and bring to a full, rolling boil. Reduce the heat to a simmer and skim off any scum that has accumulated at the top.

Let the stock simmer slowly for 18 to 20 hours, making sure not to let it boil and occasionally skimming off any scum that accumulates at the top. Never stir or mix the stock, and if the water level reduces significantly, simply add a little more cold water.

Carefully strain the stock through a fine sieve or double layer of cheesecloth into another pot. Place this pot over medium heat and bring the stock to a boil. Let the stock slowly reduce, skimming any scum that appears and washing down the sides of the pot with cold water and a pastry brush.

Reduce the stock by two-thirds, or until it's thick enough to coat the back of a spoon. Strain it through a fine sieve or double layer of cheesecloth again and let it cool to room temperature. Refrigerate overnight before using or freeze using the same method as described in the recipe for Basic Chicken Stock (see Index).

Yield: 4 to 5 cups

ALPHABET SOUP WITH MORELS AND FRESH HERBS

Purchase canned beef broth or make your own by using the Reduced Veal Stock recipe, replacing the veal bones with beef bones and disregarding the instructions for reducing it.

> 20 large, dried morels
> 3 quarts rich beef broth,
>   preferably homemade
> 2¼ cups alphabet noodles
> 1½ pounds lean beef trimmings or
>   beef stew meat
> Salt and freshly ground black
>   pepper to taste
> 1 tablespoon each chopped fresh
>   chives, rosemary, thyme,
>   parsley, tarragon, and sage

Rehydrate the morels in the hot beef broth. Drain and reserve both the morels and the broth. Cook the alphabet noodles according to package directions until al dente. Drain and reserve.

Trim all visible fat from the meat and cut into ¼-inch dice. Put the beef broth in a soup pot and bring to a boil. Add the meat and simmer slowly for 7 minutes. Add the reserved morels and noodles and return to a boil. Season to taste with salt and pepper and garnish with the chopped herbs.

Yield: 10 servings

SIMPLE CREAM OF ASPARAGUS SOUP

Use this recipe to make any cream soup simply by replacing the asparagus with the vegetable of your choice.

> 2 quarts Basic Chicken Stock (see Index)
> 2¼ to 2¾ pounds fresh asparagus (5 cups grated)
> ½ medium onion, chopped fine
> ½ cup heavy cream
> Salt to taste
> Freshly ground white pepper to taste
> 4 tablespoons sour cream
> 8 asparagus tips, blanched

Bring the chicken stock to a full, rolling boil in a large saucepan. Grate the asparagus by hand or in a food processor.

Add the asparagus and the onion to the stock and return to a full boil. Reduce the heat and simmer for 15 to 20 minutes.

Puree the soup on high speed in a blender or food processor in small batches until smooth and velvety. Place back on the heat and add the cream. Heat just to a simmer but do not boil. Season to taste with salt and pepper.

Ladle the soup into four bowls and carefully lay 1 tablespoon of sour cream on each serving. Carefully lay two asparagus tips on top of the sour cream in each bowl and serve immediately.

Yield: 2 quarts (4 servings)

CORN CHOWDER WITH FRESH HERBS
AND COUNTRY-SMOKED HAM

This chowder is unusual, as it is thickened naturally with vegetables instead of with flour. This makes for a much lighter soup.

1 tablespoon oil or bacon fat
2 baking potatoes, peeled and sliced thin
1½ cups canned corn with juice
1 medium carrot, peeled and sliced thin
½ small onion, peeled and diced fine
1 quart Basic Chicken Stock (see Index)
1 cup heavy cream
1 chicken bouillon cube
1 bay leaf
Fresh thyme, tarragon, and parsley bouquet (tied loosely in cheesecloth)
½ teaspoon coarsely ground black pepper

GARNISH
2 canned pimientos, drained and diced fine
1 baking potato, peeled and diced ¼ inch thick
2 cups canned corn, drained
Salt and freshly ground black pepper to taste
¼ pound smoked ham of your choice, julienned
2 tablespoons chopped fresh herbs: thyme, tarragon, and parsley

40

Heat the oil or bacon fat in a large heavy-bottomed pot. Add the sliced potatoes, corn and juice, carrot, and onion. Sauté for 5 minutes or until slightly tender. Add the chicken stock, cream, bouillon cube, bay leaf, herb bouquet, and pepper. Bring to a boil and reduce to a simmer.

Simmer for about 1 hour, or until all the vegetables are very soft and mushy. Remove the herb bouquet. Puree in a blender or food processor until the mixture is smooth and velvety. Return the soup to the pot and add the pimientos, the diced potato, and the corn. Cook for another 30 minutes, until the potatoes are tender.

Season to taste with salt and pepper. Serve individually in bowls garnished with the julienned ham and the chopped fresh herbs.

Yield: 2 quarts (8 servings)

WARM APPLE AND SAGE
SAUSAGE TURNOVERS WITH
CIDER-CRANBERRY GLAZE

Although this recipe should be started at least one day in advance, it is fairly simple to prepare. Puff pastry sheets should be available at your local supermarket in the freezer section or from your local bakery. If you like you can freeze the turnovers unbaked and use them at a later date. This makes preparing for a dinner party a little easier.

2 pounds ground pork shoulder
1 tablespoon finely crumbled
 dried sage
½ teaspoon ground clove
¾ teaspoon coarsely ground black
 pepper
1 tablespoon crushed red pepper
¼ tablespoon ground allspice
⅓ teaspoon Worcestershire sauce
Dash Tabasco
2 tablespoons unsalted butter
4 Granny Smith apples, peeled
 and diced small
1 medium onion, chopped fine
¼ cup sour cream
2 eggs, beaten
1 sheet puff pastry, 8″ × 10″
 (about 1 pound)
2 eggs, beaten
2 tablespoons half-and-half

1 recipe Cider-Cranberry Glaze
 (recipe follows)

In a bowl combine the ground pork, sage, clove, black pepper, red pepper, allspice, Worcestershire sauce, and Tabasco. Mix well by hand to incorporate all the ingredients evenly.

Heat a large sauté pan. Add the sausage mixture and cook for 15 to 20 minutes, until all the meat is cooked and the fat has been rendered. Place the meat in a strainer or colander and allow the fat to drain from the meat. Set the meat aside and allow to cool.

Heat another sauté pan over medium heat and melt the butter. Add the diced apple and onion and cook until soft but not mushy. Remove and let cool. Add to the reserved sausage mixture.

Combine the sour cream and eggs and mix well. Add to the sausage mixture. Chill well, preferably overnight.

Preheat the oven to 350°F. Lay out the puff pastry on a table and cut it evenly into three rectangles. Cut each rectangle in half diagonally to make six triangles.

Combine the beaten eggs and the half-and-half and generously brush the top side of the puff-pastry triangles. Arrange the triangles so that one point is at the top. Place ¾ to 1 cup of the sausage mixture in the middle of each triangle.

Carefully, without spilling any of the filling, bring each bottom corner up to the top corner. Crimp the edges well all around. Brush the top of each turnover with the egg wash and put each on an ungreased baking sheet. Bake in the center of the preheated oven for 15 to 20 minutes, until the dough is golden brown and crispy. Serve each turnover immediately in a pool of Cider-Cranberry Glaze.

Yield: 6 servings

Continued on next page

CIDER-CRANBERRY GLAZE

2 shallots, chopped fine
2 cups apple cider
2 tablespoons applejack
1 tablespoon apple-cider vinegar
¼ teaspoon whole cloves
1 cup fresh or frozen cranberries
2 tablespoons cornstarch
2 tablespoons cool water
Salt to taste
Freshly ground white pepper to
taste

Combine the shallots, apple cider, applejack, vinegar, and cloves in a medium saucepan. Bring to a boil over medium heat.

Add the cranberries and simmer until all the berries have broken, about 20 minutes. Combine the cornstarch and cool water and mix well.

Add the cornstarch mixture to the cranberry mixture and whisk to dissolve. Cook 5 more minutes over medium heat, stirring constantly.

Remove from the heat and puree in a blender until smooth. Strain through a fine sieve or cheesecloth. Season with the salt and pepper and serve hot.

Yield: 6 servings

SAVORY BREAD PUDDING
WITH SMOKED DUCK

I love bread puddings. This appetizer adapts the basic bread-pudding concept, but it is savory rather than sweet.

½ cup dry white wine
2 tablespoons chopped fresh
   tarragon
1 tablespoon fresh thyme leaves
1 clove garlic, chopped fine
1¾ cups heavy cream
7 eggs, beaten
½ teaspoon ground nutmeg
Salt to taste
Freshly ground white pepper to
   taste
2 tablespoons unsalted butter
3 cups mushrooms, sliced thin
¼ cup Reduced Veal Stock (see
   Index)
12 slices good white bread
1 pound spinach, cleaned,
   stemmed, and blanched
½ pound smoked duck breast,
   sliced very thin

1 recipe Tomato Aspic (see Index)
1 recipe Creamy Leek Puree
   (recipe follows)

Preheat the oven to 350°F. Grease an 11½" × 3¼" terrine mold well and line the sides and bottom with parchment paper. In a medium saucepan combine ¼ cup of the wine, tarragon, thyme, and garlic. Bring to a boil over medium heat; lower the heat and reduce the liquid slowly until almost dry.

Continued on next page

Add the cream and bring to a boil, stirring continuously. Remove from the heat and let cool completely. Add the eggs and, using a wire whisk, whip well. Pass the custard through a fine sieve or cheesecloth. Add the nutmeg and season to taste with salt and pepper. Set aside.

Melt the butter in a medium sauté pan over high heat and add the mushrooms. Brown them well and deglaze the pan with the remaining ¼ cup white wine. Add the veal stock and toss the mushrooms until well coated. Set them aside to cool.

Trim the crust from three slices of bread. Dip the bread into the reserved custard and let it soak for approximately 30 seconds. Carefully line the bottom of the terrine evenly with the bread.

Dry the spinach well and evenly distribute it over the top of the bread. Trim and soak three more bread slices in the custard and place them on top of the spinach. Carefully add the sliced, smoked duck and distribute evenly. Repeat with another layer of bread. Evenly distribute the reserved, sliced mushrooms to form the sixth layer. Repeat with the remaining three bread slices to form the final layer of the terrine. Pour any remaining custard over the top of the terrine. Cover with a well-greased piece of parchment paper and wrap the entire terrine in plastic wrap.

Place in a water bath (deep baking dish half filled with warm water) and bake on the middle rack of the preheated oven for 40 to 45 minutes, or until firm to the touch and registering 140°F on a regular meat thermometer placed in the center of the terrine. Cool the terrine for 1 to 2 hours, until it reaches room temperature.

Place a weight on top of the terrine. (You can use a cookie sheet pan and a few heavy cans.) Refrigerate, with weights, overnight, and then slice. Serve warmed with Tomato Aspic and Creamy Leek Puree.

Yield: 1 terrine (10 to 12 servings)

CREAMY LEEK PUREE
1 cup Basic Chicken Stock (see
    Index)
4 leeks
4 tablespoons white rice
¼ cup heavy cream
Salt to taste
Freshly ground black pepper to
    taste

Put the chicken stock in a medium saucepan and bring to a full, rolling boil over medium heat.

In the meantime, prepare the leeks by slicing off the roots and cutting off the dark green tops and discarding them. Slice the leeks as fine as possible. Rinse well under cold water. Let drain and pat dry with paper towels. Add the leeks and rice to the chicken stock and cook, covered, over medium heat for approximately 20 minutes, until the leeks are soft enough to puree.

Place the mixture in a blender or food processor and process until smooth and velvety. Add the cream and season to taste with the salt and pepper.

Yield: 1½ cups (6 servings)

CHILLED HAM-PEAR LOAF
WITH THREE-BERRY RELISH

The smoky flavor of the ham is enhanced by the sweetness of the pears and the tartness of the Three-Berry Relish. Make sure to start this a day ahead of time so the loaf will be well chilled and easy to slice. To weigh the loaf down, place it, wrapped in plastic wrap, in the refrigerator and place a clean cookie sheet on top. Place a few heavy cans on top of the cookie sheet and let it sit overnight. This will compress the meat so that as it cools it will become firm and dense.

½ pound smoked ham, cut into
strips ½" × ½" × 4"
4 cups cold water
⅓ cup dried cherries
¼ cup ruby port
1¾ pounds lean ground pork
shoulder
¼ pound beef suet, diced fine
¼ pound pork fatback, diced fine
½ cup heavy cream
¼ cup brandy
2 eggs, beaten
3 pears, peeled, cored, and diced
¼ cup apple cider
¼ cup dry white wine
1 clove garlic, minced fine
½ tablespoon plus ¼ teaspoon salt
3 teaspoons freshly ground black
pepper
¼ teaspoon ground nutmeg
½ teaspoon ground allspice
2 tablespoons chopped fresh
chives
¼ pound sliced bacon

1 recipe Three-Berry Relish (see
Index)

Chill the work bowl and metal blade of a food processor well. Soak the ham in the water for 1½ hours; soak the cherries in the ruby port for 1½ hours. Drain the ham and discard the water; drain the cherries and reserve the port and the cherries. Set aside.

In the bowl of the food processor, puree the pork shoulder, beef suet, and fatback. Once the mixture is smooth, add the port and cream gradually. Process until well mixed, smooth, and velvety. Set aside.

In a saucepan on the stove, flame the brandy and set it aside to cool.

In a large bowl, combine the pork mixture, eggs, pears, apple cider, white wine, garlic, salt, pepper, nutmeg, allspice, chives, reserved brandy, and dried cherries.

Preheat the oven to 300°F. Line a 11½″ × 3¼″ terrine mold with the bacon strips. Put about one-quarter of the mixture on the bottom of the terrine and lay one-third of the smoked ham strips on top. Repeat this two more times and cover the final layer of ham with the remaining meat mixture.

Cover the top with bacon strips. Cover the top of the mold with a double layer of aluminum foil. Place the terrine in a water bath (a deep baking dish half filled with warm water) and place in the preheated oven. Bake for 2 hours and remove the foil. Bake for 30 minutes more, or until the internal temperature of the terrine reaches 160°F. Remove from the water bath and let cool to room temperature. Refrigerate overnight, weighted down with a cookie pan. Slice and serve well chilled with Three-Berry Relish.

Yield: 1 loaf (10 to 12 servings)

HAM-AND-CHEESE FRITTERS IN CRANBERRY CUSTARD SAUCE

These fritters are one of the most popular appetizers at Prairie. They are a classic combination of flavors—ham, cheese, yams, and cranberries—uniquely prepared and delicious to eat.

> ½ pound smoked ham, fully
> cooked
> ½ pound smoked Gouda or
> cheddar cheese
> 4 tablespoons pureed yams (see
> Note)
> 1 recipe Fritter Batter (see
> Broccoli Fritters with Cheddar
> Hollandaise in Index)
>
> 1 recipe Cranberry Custard Sauce
> (recipe follows)

Slice the ham and the cheese very thin. Divide the ham evenly into four piles. Repeat with the cheese.

Carefully layer the ham and cheese alternately while spreading a little of the pureed yam between the slices. Repeat until all the piles have been used.

Carefully pick up each bundle and gently form it into a ball in the palms of your hands. Secure each ball using two or three toothpicks. Chill well for 2 to 3 hours.

Remove from the refrigerator and gently dip the balls into the fritter batter. Deep-fry at 350°F until golden brown all over, about 6 to 8 minutes.

Remove and drain well on paper towels. Remove the toothpicks. Serve hot with Cranberry Custard Sauce on the side.

Note: To make 1½ cups pureed yams use 1½ pounds whole untrimmed yams. Peel them and remove any bruises or bad spots. Cut into 1-inch chunks and place in a medium-sized saucepan. Cover with water and bring to a boil. Boil until very soft and drain well in a colander. Puree while still hot in a food processor fitted with a steel blade.

Yield: 4 servings

CRANBERRY CUSTARD SAUCE

1 cup cranberries
¼ cup red-wine vinegar
⅓ cup granulated sugar
2 sprigs fresh tarragon
¼ teaspoon whole black
   peppercorns
1 bay leaf
3 egg yolks
1 egg, beaten
2 tablespoons water
Pinch salt
Freshly ground white pepper to
   taste

In a medium saucepan, combine the cranberries, vinegar, sugar, tarragon, peppercorns, and bay leaf. Bring the mixture to a boil over medium heat, stirring constantly. Reduce the heat and simmer until all the berries have broken, approximately 15 minutes. Set aside and let cool.

In a stainless-steel bowl fitted over a double boiler, combine the egg yolks, egg, water, salt, and pepper. Using a wire whisk, whip the eggs vigorously until they hold soft peaks.

Remove from the heat and add the reserved cranberry mixture. Stir well to combine. Pass the sauce through a fine sieve or double layer of cheesecloth and keep warm until ready to serve.

Yield: 3 cups (6 servings)

BRANDIED GAME LOAF

Although this is not the easiest preparation, or the cheapest, it certainly feeds a lot of people and is perfect for a large dinner or hors d'oeuvre party. It is an elegant presentation of pieces of meat laced in a smooth, creamy forcemeat (flavored with a hint of brandy) and wrapped in bacon. When served with the plum catsup it tastes as delicious as it looks.

GARNISH

1 pound skinless pheasant or chicken breast, diced large

¼ pound smoked ham, diced large

¼ pound skinless duck breast, diced large

¼ pound skinless turkey breast, diced large

¼ pound rabbit sausage meatballs (see Note) about 1 inch in diameter

1 cup brandy

½ pound mushrooms, quartered

½ cup kale, shredded, blanched, and drained

3 tablespoons chopped fresh chives

1 tablespoon salt

1 tablespoon freshly ground black pepper

LOAF

¾ pound lean, boneless pork shoulder

½ pound fatback, no skin

1 teaspoon salt

1 tablespoon freshly ground white pepper

1 teaspoon chopped fresh thyme

2 cloves garlic, minced fine

6 juniper berries, crushed

½ cup brandy
1 egg
¾ pound bacon, to line terrine
5 to 6 bay leaves

Prairie Plum Catsup (see Index)

To make the garnish, quickly sauté the pheasant/chicken, ham, duck, turkey, and rabbit sausage, browning them very well on all sides. (Do this in small batches in a very hot pan.) Flame each batch with a small amount of brandy. Drain the fat well and chill.

Repeat the same process for the mushrooms. Combine the meats, mushrooms, kale, and chives in a bowl and season well with salt and pepper. Set aside.

To make the game loaf, preheat the oven to 375°F. Cut the pork and fatback into strips. Place in a shallow, stainless-steel pan and season with the salt, white pepper, thyme, garlic, and juniper berries. Cover well with plastic wrap and chill 3 to 4 hours. Grind the meat through a meat grinder set on medium. Chill the mixture and grind again.

Over a bowl of ice, mix the fat and the meat thoroughly. It is important that the meat be well chilled throughout the preparation.

Fold the garnish mixture into the ground meat mixture. Add the brandy and egg. Test for seasoning. Line a 11½″ × 3¼″ terrine mold with the bacon, allowing the strips to hang over the top. Put the forcemeat into the mold and cover with the overhanging bacon.

Top with the bay leaves and cover well with aluminum foil. Place the terrine in a water bath (a deep baking dish half-filled with warm water) and put in the preheated oven. Bake for about 2 hours, or until the internal temperature reaches about 170°F. Remove the foil about 1½ hours into the cooking process.

Refrigerate with a weight (place a cookie sheet and a few heavy cans over it) overnight. Slice and serve chilled with Prairie Plum Catsup (see Index).

Note: See Wild Game, Inc., in Sources for Midwest Specialties for rabbit sausage.

Yield: 12 servings

REGIONAL MUSHROOM SAUTE IN AN ONION-DILL BISCUIT WITH MOREL PUREE

If the mushrooms listed are not available, you may substitute other varieties.

MUSHROOM MIXTURE
Butter or vegetable oil for
    sautéing
½ pound button mushrooms,
    sliced very thin
¼ pound oyster mushrooms,
    halved
¼ pound white trumpet
    mushrooms, whole
¼ pound morels, quartered
Salt and freshly ground black
    pepper to taste

ONION-DILL BISCUITS
1½ tablespoons dry yeast
½ cup warm water
2½ tablespoons granulated sugar
1 tablespoon onion, diced fine
2 tablespoons unsalted butter,
    melted
1 tablespoon salt
1 tablespoon chopped fresh dill
1 teaspoon baking soda
1 egg, beaten
1 tablespoon prepared horseradish
1 pound small-curd cottage cheese
4⅓ cups all-purpose flour
3 to 4 tablespoons melted butter

MOREL PUREE
1 pound fresh morels, cleaned (or
    substitute button mushrooms)
4 shallots, peeled and minced fine
2 sprigs fresh thyme
2 sprigs fresh tarragon

¼ cup white wine
1 quart Basic Chicken Stock (see
  Index)
1 cup heavy cream
Salt and freshly ground black
  pepper to taste

GARNISH
Chopped fresh chives
Sour cream

Preheat the oven to 350°F. Grease 8 muffin cups well. Pick over the mushrooms and clean them well. Reserve.

Combine the yeast, water, and sugar and let rest for 10 minutes, until foamy. Add the onion, 2 tablespoons of butter, salt, dill, baking soda, egg, horseradish, and cottage cheese. Mix well.

Add the flour all at once, stirring to make a smooth dough. Turn out onto a floured board and knead for 5 to 7 minutes. Put the dough in a greased bowl and turn to coat the surface of the dough. Cover and let rise in a warm, moist place until double in volume, approximately 35 to 40 minutes. Punch the dough down and divide into 1-ounce biscuits, approximately the size of silver dollars. Place the biscuits in the muffin cups and brush with melted butter. Bake in the preheated oven until golden brown, about 20 to 30 minutes.

While the biscuits are rising and baking, make the puree and prepare the mushroom mixture. For the puree, sweat the morels, shallots, and fresh herbs in a medium-sized, covered saucepan for 6 to 7 minutes. Add the white wine and reduce until almost dry. Add the chicken stock and reduce by half. Add the cream and puree very well in a blender or food processor until smooth and velvety. Add the salt and pepper. Puree should be just thick enough to coat the back of a spoon.

In a very hot pan, using a small amount of butter or vegetable oil, sauté the mushrooms until well colored, about 3 to 4 minutes. Season to taste with salt and pepper.

To serve, put a small pool of morel puree on a plate. Split a biscuit in half and put one half on the pool of sauce. Top this with some of the sautéed mushrooms and then with the other biscuit half. Garnish with the chopped chives and sour cream.

Yield: 8 servings

SMOKED TROUT TERRINE

The pike in this recipe is used to bind and lighten the terrine, while the smoked trout (see Green River Trout Farm in Sources for Midwest Specialties) is used as the main flavor component. Remember to make it a day in advance (as with all terrines) and serve with the subtle Horseradish-Dill Mayonnaise to bring out the flavor of the smoked trout.

> 20 2-ounce pieces smoked brook
>   trout
> ⅓ cup dry white wine
> Juice of 1 lemon
> Salt and freshly ground black
>   pepper to taste
> 1 pound boneless and skinless
>   pike fillets
> ¼ cup fresh, white bread crumbs
> 2 egg yolks
> ⅓ cup unsalted butter
> ⅓ cup heavy cream
> 2 tablespoons vegetable oil
> 1 pound spinach, cleaned and
>   stemmed
> Unsalted softened butter to line
>   terrine
> 1 cup pimientos, drained and
>   diced fine
> 5 bay leaves
>
> 3 cups Horseradish-Dill
>   Mayonnaise (recipe follows)

Preheat the oven to 325°F. Remove the bones and skin from the trout, saving the meat and fat. Reserve about one-third of the biggest, nicest pieces.

Using your fingers, shred the remaining two-thirds of the smoked trout and fat into a stainless-steel bowl and add the wine, lemon juice, salt, and freshly ground pepper. Toss the mixture gently and allow to marinate for 2 hours in the refrigerator, tossing from time to time.

Chill the bowl and blade of your food processor for about 30 minutes in a bowl of icewater. Process the raw pike in the processor until very smooth. Add the bread crumbs, egg yolks, ⅓ cup butter, and cream. Process until very smooth. Add the marinated trout and juices and incorporate very quickly. *Do not overprocess* at this point—just process enough to combine the ingredients.

Heat the oil in a large skillet or frying pan over high heat. Add the spinach and stir quickly, just until bright green and wilted. Remove, chill well, and chop rough.

Butter an 11½" × 3¼" terrine mold with the softened butter and line with parchment paper on all sides as well as the bottom. Gently fold the diced pimientos and chilled spinach into the forcemeat and season to taste with salt and pepper. Fill the terrine with the forcemeat while layering alternately with the whole pieces of smoked trout. Place the five whole bay leaves across the top of the terrine; cover with buttered parchment paper and then with foil. Place in a water bath (a deep baking dish half filled with warm water) in the preheated oven and bake for 45 minutes. Cool on a rack for 1 to 2 hours at room temperature. Weight down the top of the terrine (place a cookie sheet and a few heavy cans over it) and refrigerate overnight. Serve sliced and chilled with Horseradish-Dill Mayonnaise.

Yield: Approximately 12 servings

Continued on next page

HORSERADISH-DILL MAYONNAISE

1½ cups mayonnaise, preferably
   homemade (see Perfect
   Mayonnaise in Index)
Juice of 2 lemons
1 bunch freshly chopped dill,
   no stems
¼ cup dry white wine
3 tablespoons prepared
   horseradish

Combine all of the ingredients and mix well. Refrigerate until needed. Serve at room temperature. If the mixture is too thick, thin with a little cool water.

Yield: 2 cups (approximately 8 servings)

SALADS, CONDIMENTS, AND RELISHES

Salads are offered on Prairie's menu before the main course or entree, as is customary in this country. Many of these salads make satisfying meals, when accompanied by good bread and a glass of wine. Many are variations on traditional favorites like potato salad; Prairie offers two of these. You'll find a chef's salad with some unusual ingredients that are prepared right in Prairie's kitchen and the recipes for which can be found in this chapter. There are some new salads, too, like the Chilled Asparagus Salad with Rhubarb Mayonnaise.

Attention to detail is Prairie's hallmark, and this is reflected in the offering of condiments and relishes that were created as complements to specific dishes on the menu but are versatile enough to go with any similar dishes. These condiments and relishes have their roots in the canning tradition that arose as a response to lack of refrigeration in the early settlers' time. The modern versions have been revised to eliminate the strong acidity originally necessary to preserve these foods.

We even commissioned a Chicago ceramics artist, Erin McNamara, to create appropriate dishes in which to serve the "homemade" Roasted Red Pepper-Corn Relish and Pear-Honey Chutney. But don't worry: They will taste just as good served at home in your own dishes.

CANNING BASICS

Canning, or "putting up," has been practiced by homemakers in the heartland for years. Rewarding and cost-effective, canning requires only some careful advance preparation and a little time and effort to produce good results. To a seasoned canner the process seems effortless, but extreme care must always be exercised to avoid contamination and spoilage. Therefore, it is imperative that you follow closely the manufacturer's instructions for the particular type of jar you use and also that you consult a reliable canning book. For added fun and safety, have an experienced canner walk you through the whole process, especially if you are a beginner. For your convenience, here is an overview of canning procedures.

Canning jars come in half-pint, pint, and quart sizes, so refer to the yield listed for the particular recipe. It is best to use mason-type jars with screw bands and dome lids so that the seals may be more easily checked after processing. Be sure that you have the right size bands and lids for the mouths of the jars you will be using. Before even beginning the canning process, assemble all your equipment and check the jars and lids for cracks or other damage that may lead to improper sealing. Do not use decorative jars or lids—they will not withstand processing or seal properly. Some additional pointers:

- Decide in advance what you will need and have it all out and ready to use
- Use only glass, enamel, or stainless-steel bowls and containers for mixing
- Be careful to avoid sudden temperature changes that could crack jars
- Keep sterilized jars, lids, and bands hot until you are ready to use them
- Use only nonmetal utensils to fill the jars or to remove air bubbles or food from them
- Clean up as you go along

Preparing the Jars and Processing Them

Sterilize the jars, screw bands, and lids (note that the lids can be used *only once*) by covering them with water and boiling them for a minimum of 15 minutes. Keep the jars, bands, and lids in hot water, gently simmering, until they are ready to be used. When it's time to fill the jars, remove them from the water using special canning-jar tongs or wearing rubber gloves, and transfer them to a clean towel. Let the jars drain momentarily, then fill them while the food product is still very hot. An easy way to fill the jars is to fill them with solid food first, and then, using a funnel, pour in the liquid, leaving a ¼-inch head space. Remove any air bubbles by running a specially made plastic bubble freer, or any other nonmetal kitchen utensil, through the mixture in each jar. Wipe any spillage with a clean towel, making sure that the rim and threads on the neck of the jar are clean. Now remove the lids from the hot water, pat them dry with a clean towel, and place them on top of the jars. Remove the screw bands from the water, place them on the necks of the jars, and twist, by hand only, to tighten.

Processing is next. The filled jars should now be placed into a rack in a deep, large pot (boiling water-bath canners with racks are commercially available) that contains enough boiling water to cover the jars by at least 1 to 2 inches. Cover the pot, bring the water back to a full, rolling boil, and continue boiling for 15 to 20 minutes. After boiling, immediately remove the jars to a rack or a layer of towels for cooling. Space them at least 1 to 2

inches apart. When the jars have thoroughly cooled, the lids can be examined for proper sealing. If the lid is slightly depressed in the center, the seal is good. (You may have heard slight "pings" as the jars were cooling—an indication that sealing was taking place.) If the lid is slightly elevated, press it down; if it comes back up, the jar isn't sealed and should either be promptly reprocessed using a new lid (since the old one is now no good and should be thrown away) or refrigerated and used before the contents spoil. After determining that the seals are good, the screw bands can be removed. Wash off any food residue on the jar with warm, soapy water, and dry by hand before storing. Jars can be cooled for 12 to 24 hours before labeling and storing. Make sure to check the seals on the jars once again before you open them.

PRAIRIE CHEF'S SALAD

A mixture of lettuces and spinach combined with an assortment of mid-western cheeses and smoked meats make this salad a meal in itself. It goes particularly well with the Creamy Vegetable Dressing but can be served with any of the dressings listed in this chapter.

1 head red leaf lettuce
2 heads Boston lettuce
¼ pound spinach, cleaned and
    stemmed
2 leaves Batavian or curly endive,
    shredded
¼ pound crumbled blue cheese,
    preferably Nauvoo or Maytag
1 small rutabaga, julienned fine
¼ pound sharp cheddar cheese,
    julienned fine
¼ pound smoked turkey breast,
    julienned
6 hard-boiled eggs, chopped
¼ pound smoked ham, julienned
    fine
1 small red onion, sliced fine
1 cup Miniature Mix (see Index)

Wash and pick over the salad greens well, discarding all the bruised leaves. Cut into bite-size pieces and drain well. Dry in a salad spinner.

Divide the greens evenly onto four plates. Sprinkle the other ingredients over the greens. Serve immediately with a choice of dressings.

Yield: 4 servings

CHILLED ASPARAGUS SALAD
WITH RHUBARB MAYONNAISE

The tanginess of the rhubarb mayonnaise provides an interesting flavor contrast to the crisp asparagus. Flowering cole, also known as ornamental cabbage, is white or purple in color and descends from the kale family. It is usually available at supermarkets or gourmet food stores.

40 asparagus spears, preferably
very thin, "pencil" type

RHUBARB MAYONNAISE
1 cup washed and thinly sliced
rhubarb
¼ cup red-wine vinegar
¼ cup granulated sugar
Juice of 2 lemons
1 sprig fresh thyme
1 cup good mayonnaise,
preferably homemade (see
Perfect Mayonnaise in Index)
Pinch salt
Pinch freshly ground white pepper

4 leaves purple flowering cole
4 leaves white flowering cole
4 leaves green kale
4 leaves baby lettuce

In a large saucepan bring a good amount of water to a full, rolling boil. Tie the asparagus together in bunches of ten, making sure the tips are all even. Trim the stem bottoms, making sure to cut off all the tough, brown, dry parts.

Prepare the ice-water bath using plenty of ice and cold water. Plunge the asparagus bunches into the boiling water and boil uncovered for 10 to 15 minutes, or until the asparagus is bright green and cooked al dente.

Remove the asparagus from the water very carefully, using a pair of tongs, and plunge directly into the ice-water bath. Drain well and reserve.

To make the rhubarb mayonnaise, combine the rhubarb, vinegar, sugar, lemon juice, and thyme in a small, nonreactive saucepan. Cook over very low heat for about 30 minutes, or until the rhubarb becomes soft and mushy. In a blender, blend the mixture on high speed until it is smooth and velvety. Let cool.

Again using the blender, combine the rhubarb mixture with the mayonnaise and blend until smooth on medium or low speed. Season to taste with salt and pepper, and adjust the consistency with a little cold water, if necessary. Chill well.

Arrange the purple cole, white cole, kale, and baby lettuce on a salad plate. Place ten spears or a bundle of asparagus on top of each. Serve the rhubarb mayonnaise on the side.

Yield: 4 servings

FRIED CHICKEN AND BABY LETTUCE SALAD

This is suitable as a main-course salad for lunch or an appetizer salad at dinner. Try experimenting with different lettuces and greens you may find at your local farmers' market. Make sure to serve the salad while the chicken is still hot for a nice combination of temperatures, textures, and flavors.

4 heads baby Lolla Rossa lettuce
2 heads baby oak-leaf lettuce
6 leaves baby Bibb lettuce
4 bunches lamb's lettuce
1 cup all-purpose flour
2 tablespoons Hungarian paprika
1 teaspoon dried oregano
1 teaspoon salt
½ teaspoon freshly ground black pepper
2 pounds skinless, boneless chicken breasts
5 eggs, beaten
Oil for deep frying
1 red bell pepper, sliced thin
1 green bell pepper, sliced thin
1 cup Garlic-Herb Vinegar Dressing (see Index)

Wash and carefully pick over the lettuces, discarding any bruised leaves. (If any of the particular types listed above is not available, you may substitute another type or simply use Bibb or Boston lettuce.) Drain the lettuces well and spin dry in a salad spinner. Cut into bite-size pieces and set aside.

In a bowl, combine the flour, paprika, oregano, salt, and pepper. Cut the chicken breasts into ¼-inch strips. Dredge them well in the egg, then in the seasoned flour. Deep-fry the strips for 6 to 8 minutes, until golden brown and cooked through. Remove the chicken strips and drain well on paper towels.

While the chicken cooks, toss the greens in the Garlic-Herb Vinegar Dressing to coat well. Arrange on four plates. Arrange the chicken pieces evenly over the greens. Garnish the salad by arranging the pepper strips over the chicken. Serve immediately.

Yield: 4 servings

GRILLED DUCK BREAST SALAD
WITH HONEY-THYME VINEGAR

Great as an appetizer or served by itself as a light lunch.

> 2 double duck breasts
> 2 heads Boston lettuce
> 4 leaves purple flowering cole
>   (ornamental cabbage)
> 4 leaves white flowering cole
>   (ornamental cabbage)
> ½ cup Root-Vegetable Relish Mix
>   (see Index)
> 1 cup Honey-Thyme Vinegar (see
>   Index)

Using a sharp knife, split the duck breasts down the middle and carefully remove the skin. Cut the skin into small dice. Place the diced skin in a medium sauté pan and cook over low heat to render all the fat. Continue cooking for 20 to 25 minutes, until all the fat has been rendered out and the skin is golden brown and crispy. Be careful, for the fat will get extremely hot and will splatter if it comes into contact with the slightest bit of water.

Strain the fat from the skin using a strainer. Discard the fat and reserve the cracklings (the crispy skin). Cook the duck breasts on a grill or under a broiler for about 6 minutes on each side. Remove and let rest for 3 to 4 minutes.

Clean and pick over the lettuce, discarding any bruised leaves. Rinse well and dry in a salad spinner. Cut into bite-size pieces and divide evenly among four plates. Garnish the tops of the plates with the flowering cole leaves.

Slice the duck breasts lengthwise as thin as possible (an electric knife works best for this) and arrange over the greens. Allow a single breast per salad.

Pour warmed Honey-Thyme Vinegar over each serving, sprinkle with the marinated root vegetables and the reserved duck cracklings, and serve immediately.

Yield: 4 servings

WARM POTATO SALAD

This vinaigrette-type potato salad is best when served warm. In the summer, when I have friends over for a barbecue in the backyard, I make it and serve it with grilled brats, pickles, cucumber relish, and ice-cold beer for a light summer meal.

2 pounds russet potatoes
¼ pound finely diced bacon
1 medium onion, diced fine
1¼ tablespoons granulated sugar
1 tablespoon all-purpose flour
2 teaspoons salt
½ teaspoon freshly ground black
    pepper
¾ cup malt vinegar
¼ cup water
1 teaspoon celery seeds
3 tablespoons finely chopped fresh
    parsley

Cook the potatoes in their jackets until they are tender enough to slice. Cool and peel. Slice ½ inch thick. Cook the bacon until crispy and then add the onion. Cook until the onion becomes transparent.

Combine the sugar, flour, salt, and pepper; blend into the bacon-onion mixture. Stir in the vinegar and water. Cook the mixture for 10 minutes, stirring constantly.

Pour over the sliced potatoes and add the celery seeds and chopped parsley. Toss very gently. Serve immediately.

Yield: About 2 pounds (4 servings)

AMISH POTATO SALAD

I once tasted a delicious potato salad at a deli in a small town in Indiana. The young lady behind the counter informed me that it was made by a woman in the Amish community down the road. I tried hard to imitate it, and I think I've come pretty close with this recipe. Basically, it's a chunky potato salad tossed in a light mustard dressing infused with bacon and celery seed.

> 10 large russet potatoes
> 1½ red bell peppers, diced
>   medium
> 1½ green bell peppers, diced
>   medium
> 1 small red onion, diced fine
> ¾ pound cooked, crumbled bacon
> 1 jar pickled baby corn
> 1 tablespoon celery seeds
> ¾ cup white wine
> ¼ cup cider vinegar
> 1 cup yellow salad-style mustard
> ¼ cup all-purpose flour
> ⅓ cup granulated sugar
> ¼ tablespoon salt
> Freshly ground white pepper to
>   taste

Peel the potatoes and cut them into large dice (1-inch cubes). Boil in plenty of water for approximately 20 minutes or until tender but not mushy. Drain well and let cool to room temperature. Toss the potatoes with the diced peppers, onion, and bacon.

Quarter the baby corn and add that to the potato mixture. Mix well and set aside. Combine the celery seeds, white wine, vinegar, mustard, flour, sugar, salt, and white pepper in a nonreactive saucepan. Cook over medium heat, stirring constantly, until well thickened, about 15 to 20 minutes. Let the dressing cool to room temperature and pour over the potato mixture. Toss gently and adjust seasonings. This is best served the next day.

Yield: 5 pounds of salad (8 to 10 servings)

WARM SPINACH SALAD WITH SLICED PORK LOIN AND APPLE-CARAWAY KRAUT

Fresh spinach and tender slices of pork are enlivened by the addition of an apple-caraway kraut. Although similar to sauerkraut, this variation combines the traditional cabbage with apple, potato, brown sugar, vinegar, and caraway seeds for more complex flavors.

> 6 strips bacon, julienned
> 1 medium onion, chopped fine
> ½ head Savoy cabbage, shredded fine
> 1 Granny Smith apple, peeled and diced fine
> ¼ cup Basic Chicken Stock (see Index)
> 2 tablespoons dry white wine
> 1 potato, peeled and grated
> ¼ cup cider vinegar
> 1 tablespoon brown sugar
> 1 tablespoon caraway seeds
> 1½ pounds fresh spinach
> 1 pound pork tenderloin
>
> GARNISH
> 1 red Delicious apple, sliced thin
> 4 hard-boiled eggs, chopped

Place the bacon in a large sauté pan over medium heat and cook to render the fat. When the bacon becomes brown and crispy, remove it from the pan, leaving behind the rendered fat. Set bacon aside.

Add the onion and sauté 5 minutes, or until transparent. Add the cabbage, cover, and simmer for 10 minutes. Add the apple, chicken stock, wine, potato, cider vinegar, and brown sugar. Simmer gently over medium heat until the apples and cabbage are tender but not mushy, about 10 to 12 minutes. Add the caraway seeds and set aside, keeping the mixture hot.

Wash and stem the spinach. Drain well and dry in a salad spinner. Tear the spinach into bite-size pieces. Arrange the spinach on four plates.

Cook the pork tenderloin, either by grilling it outdoors over hickory or apple wood or simply by roasting it until done, using a meat thermometer (should register 160°F). Slice the pork very thin and arrange it evenly over the spinach.

Top with the hot kraut and the juices from the kraut. Garnish with the apple slices, chopped hard-boiled eggs, and reserved bacon.

Serve immediately.

Yield: 4 servings

BLUE CHEESE DRESSING

This creamy combination of mayonnaise and sour cream with chunks of blue cheese goes well with any type of green salad or simply as a dipping sauce. Any good blue cheese will work, and Nauvoo or Maytag Blue (see Sources for Midwest Specialties) are two of the best made in this country.

> ¼ pound blue cheese, preferably
> Nauvoo or Maytag
> 2 cups good mayonnaise (see
> Perfect Mayonnaise in Index)
> ½ cup sour cream
> ¼ cup white-wine vinegar
> ¾ tablespoon red-wine vinegar
> ¾ tablespoon Worcestershire sauce
> ½ teaspoon freshly ground white
> pepper
> ½ teaspoon finely chopped garlic
> ½ teaspoon salt

Using an electric mixer or food processor fitted with a steel blade, combine all of the ingredients. Blend on low speed until smooth.

Chill overnight before using.

Yield: 1 quart

GARLIC-HERB VINEGAR DRESSING

This light, fragrant dressing is a mixture of aromatic herbs, vinegars, and oil. For a variation, try substituting different fresh herbs such as lemon balm, chives, or thyme. Don't use dried herbs, however, for they lack the flavor and character needed in this dressing.

2½ cups salad oil
¾ cup red-wine vinegar
¾ cup malt vinegar
½ bunch fresh parsley, chopped fine
½ bunch fresh cilantro, chopped fine
¼ cup dry white wine
1½ tablespoons finely minced garlic
1 tablespoon finely chopped fresh basil
1 tablespoon finely chopped fresh tarragon
½ tablespoon finely chopped fresh rosemary
½ tablespoon finely chopped fresh oregano
2 teaspoons salt
2 teaspoons freshly ground black pepper

Combine all ingredients in a bowl and whisk well. Allow to sit overnight for the flavors to meld before using.

Yield: 1 quart

HONEY-POPPYSEED DRESSING

If a restaurant is to be truly midwestern, it must serve honey-poppyseed dressing. This traditional version is just slightly sweet from the honey, and the poppyseeds offer an interesting texture when served with any salad or with crudités. I use this dressing in a coleslaw to give it a different taste.

> 2 eggs
> 2 tablespoons salad-style mustard
> 2 tablespoons honey
> ⅓ cup red-wine vinegar
> 3 cups salad oil
> Salt to taste
> Freshly ground white pepper to
>   taste
> 2 tablespoons poppyseeds

In a food processor fitted with a steel blade, combine the eggs, mustard, and honey. Blend just to mix the ingredients together.

With the machine running, alternately add the vinegar and oil very slowly to form a good emulsion. Season to taste with the salt and pepper and add the poppyseeds. Refrigerate overnight before using.

Yield: 1 quart

HONEY-THYME VINEGAR

As much a sauce as a salad dressing, this should always be served hot, drizzled over the top of a composition salad such as the Grilled Duck Breast Salad.

2 shallots, peeled and minced fine
½ cup honey
2 cups red-wine vinegar
5 sprigs fresh thyme
½ cup Reduced Veal Stock (see Index)
Salt to taste
Freshly ground black pepper to taste

Combine the shallots, honey, and vinegar in a nonreactive saucepan. Bring to a boil over medium heat and reduce to a simmer. Let reduce by half, about 14 to 16 minutes.

Pull the leaves from the stems of the fresh thyme and add the leaves to the honey mixture. Add the veal stock and reduce again by half, about 8 to 10 minutes. Season to taste with the salt and pepper.

Cool to room temperature and refrigerate overnight before using.

Yield: 1 quart

PERFECT MAYONNAISE

Didn't you ever wonder why there are no real "gourmet" mayonnaises in the grocery store along with all the "gourmet" salad dressings? Homemade mayonnaise always tastes lighter and more flavorful than the store-bought kind. Making your own is well worth the effort, but remember to keep it refrigerated at all times so it doesn't spoil.

3 egg yolks
1 whole egg
2 tablespoons lemon juice
2 tablespoons cider vinegar
½ teaspoon Worcestershire sauce
Dash Tabasco
½ teaspoon salt
Pinch freshly ground white pepper
4 cups vegetable oil

In the bowl of an electric mixer, or in a food processor fitted with a steel blade, combine the egg yolks, egg, lemon juice, vinegar, Worcestershire sauce, Tabasco, salt, and white pepper. Process until smooth.

While the machine is running, add the oil very, very slowly (drop by drop), until the mixture starts to thicken. During this process, be sure the mixture does not become too thick or shiny. If it does, add a little more vinegar or water to thin it. Make sure to scrape down the sides of the bowl periodically.

Continue to add the oil very slowly until all the oil has been fully incorporated into the mixture. Remove and place in a nonreactive container. Refrigerate when not using.

Yield: 1 quart

CREAMY VEGETABLE DRESSING

I wanted an unusual and appealing dressing to use as Prairie's house dressing, and this is what I came up with. It is a creamy, light, orange-tinted salad dressing with an interesting and complex flavor brought out by the ground vegetables. Use it as a perfect complement for the Prairie Chef's Salad.

1 red bell pepper, seeded
2 hard-boiled eggs, peeled
½ medium onion, peeled and
    quartered
1 rib celery
1 medium carrot, peeled
2 tablespoons chopped fresh
    parsley
2 cloves garlic, peeled
1 medium cucumber, peeled and
    seeded
2 dashes Worcestershire sauce
Dash Tabasco
3 cups mayonnaise
¼ cup red-wine vinegar
½ tablespoon granulated sugar
1 tablespoon salt
½ tablespoon freshly ground black
    pepper

Using a meat grinder or food processor fitted with a grater attachment, process the bell pepper, eggs, onion, celery, carrot, parsley, garlic, and cucumber. Place in a strainer and let drain well, about 20 minutes. Reserve the juices.

Combine the remaining ingredients in the bowl of an electric mixer fitted with a whip and mix well on high speed. Add the ground vegetables and ¼ cup of the reserved juices.

Mix well and refrigerate overnight before using.

Yield: 1 quart

APPLE BUTTER

There is nothing like a good homemade apple butter. Even though there is no butter at all in it, I have always believed that you can serve apple butter anywhere in place of butter. It's great on bread, muffins, pancakes, and even as an accompaniment to turkey or pork. There are many different types of apples available nowadays, so experiment to find the one you like best.

4 cups apple cider or apple juice
3 MacIntosh apples
3 Granny Smith apples
1½ cups granulated sugar
1 tablespoon ground cinnamon
1 teaspoon ground nutmeg
½ teaspoon ground clove
¼ teaspoon salt

Place the cider or apple juice in a heavy-bottomed, medium-sized saucepan. Bring to a full, rolling boil. Boil for 10 minutes.

Peel, core, and slice the apples. Add them to the boiling cider, reduce the heat, and simmer slowly until the apples are very soft.

Remove the mixture from the heat and puree in a blender or food processor on high speed until smooth. Return the mixture to the pan and add the sugar, cinnamon, nutmeg, clove, and salt. Simmer slowly for 15 to 20 minutes, stirring constantly to avoid burning.

Remove from the heat and allow the mixture to cool to room temperature. Place in a nonreactive container and refrigerate overnight.

Yield: 1 quart

HOMEMADE BARBECUE SAUCE

This recipe should be prepared a day ahead.

> 1 medium onion, peeled and
> quartered
> 3 cloves garlic, peeled
> ½ cup vegetable oil
> 1 12-ounce bottle dark beer
> ⅔ cup herb vinegar
> 1 cup light brown sugar, packed
> ⅓ cup Worcestershire sauce
> 1 14-ounce bottle chili relish
> 1 14-ounce bottle catsup
> 2 tablespoons barbecue spice

Combine the onion, garlic, and vegetable oil in a blender or food processor fitted with a steel blade. Process until smooth and transfer to a medium-sized saucepan.

Add the remaining ingredients and stir well to combine. Bring the mixture to a boil and reduce the heat to a simmer. Simmer slowly while stirring occasionally and skimming off any foam that accumulates.

Let the sauce reduce by half, or until it is thick enough to coat the back of a spoon. Pass through a fine sieve or double layer of cheesecloth into a nonreactive container and refrigerate overnight before using.

Yield: 2 cups

BRANDIED PEACHES

Alongside the jellies, marmalades, and preserves at state and county fairs all over the country there are always some pickles and other relish-type items to be found, including these peaches. Be sure to let them sit for at least 3 to 4 days so the flavors can meld. Serve them with chicken or duck as a side dish, or slice them and serve them with a hot fudge sundae.

1½ pounds fresh peaches
1½ cups granulated sugar
1½ cups water
⅓ teaspoon ground nutmeg
½ teaspoon ground mace
1 teaspoon whole cloves
1½ teaspoons ground allspice
2 whole cinnamon sticks
2 tablespoons brandy

Fill a large stockpot with water. Bring to a full, rolling boil. Prepare an ice-water bath using plenty of ice and water.

Plunge the peaches into the boiling water and cook, uncovered, for 40 to 50 seconds. Remove and place immediately in the ice-water bath. Remove the skins from the peaches and set aside.

Place the sugar and water in a large saucepan and bring to a boil. Add the nutmeg, mace, whole cloves, allspice, and cinnamon sticks. Reduce the heat and simmer, uncovered, for 8 to 10 minutes. Carefully add the reserved peaches to the syrup and simmer for 5 more minutes, until the peaches are tender. Add brandy. If you wish, you may can the peaches at this point. (See Index for Canning Basics.)

Remove the pot from the heat and let cool to room temperature, making sure to leave the peaches in the syrup. Place the peaches, covered with syrup, in a nonreactive container and refrigerate for 3 to 4 days before using them.

Yield: 1 quart

PEAR-HONEY CHUTNEY

This flavorful condiment combines pears, raisins, and green peppers for flavor and texture contrast. The grated fresh ginger adds a delightfully refreshing twist. Be sure to let the chutney rest for 3 to 4 days in the refrigerator before using. Serve as an accompaniment to chicken, pork, or baked ham.

8 Bartlett pears
½ cup honey
Zest of 1 lemon
¾ cup lemon juice
½ cup cider vinegar
¼ cup apple cider
¼ teaspoon fresh ginger, peeled
   and grated
⅓ teaspoon cayenne pepper
1 medium green bell pepper,
   chopped fine
⅓ cup chopped onion
½ cup raisins
¼ tablespoon salt

Peel and core the pears, and cut them into 1-inch dice. Set aside.

Combine the honey, lemon zest, lemon juice, vinegar, apple cider, ginger, and cayenne in a nonreactive, medium-sized saucepan. Add the reserved pears, green pepper, onion, raisins, and salt. Bring to a boil over medium heat, covered, stirring occasionally.

Simmer for about 20 minutes, until the pears become tender. Remove from the heat and can, if desired (see Index for Canning Basics). If not, allow the mixture to cool to room temperature and place in a nonreactive container. Refrigerate for 3 to 4 days before using.

Yield: Approximately 1 pint

PICKLED MELON

It's important to slice the melon paper thin in order for the liquid to saturate it properly. This is a very light, refreshing pickle that is best served with cottage cheese as a starter or as a palate cleanser between courses. It should be prepared a day in advance.

2 medium-ripe cantaloupes
2 ripe honeydew melons
6 cups rhubarb vinegar (see Note)
7 cups granulated sugar
2½ cups water
2 tablespoons coriander seeds
2 teaspoons whole cloves
2 tablespoons coarsely broken
   cinnamon sticks

Remove the rind from the melons; seed them and slice paper thin.

Combine the vinegar, sugar, and water in a heavy, nonreactive saucepan. Loosely tie the coriander seeds, cloves, and cinnamon together in cheesecloth and add to the vinegar mixture.

Bring the mixture to a boil over medium heat until the sugar has completely dissolved. Simmer the syrup, partially covered, for 5 minutes.

Pour the hot mixture over the melon slices and chill overnight. If you wish, you may can the melon slices after pouring the hot syrup over them. (See Index for Canning Basics.) Serve well chilled with a good-quality cottage cheese (see Cottage Cheese in Index).

Note: Rhubarb vinegar is available through Alyce's Herbs (see Sources for Midwest Specialties).

Yield: 2 quarts (6 to 8 servings)

PRAIRIE PLUM CATSUP

This catsup is similar to tomato catsup in that it shares the same thick, smooth consistency. I wouldn't recommend that you put it on your fries, though. It has an elevating sweet-and-sour flavor from the citrus and the fruit preserves, while the mustard and cayenne give it a little spice. Be sure to add the port wine the following day for extra flavor. Plum catsup is great with smoked meats and especially with Brandied Game Loaf.

1 tablespoon finely minced shallot
3 tablespoons orange zest
1 teaspoon lemon zest
1 quart canned whole plums
¾ cup plum preserves
Juice of 2 medium oranges
Juice of 2 medium lemons
1 teaspoon Dijon mustard
1 teaspoon ground nutmeg
1 teaspoon ground ginger
1 teaspoon cayenne pepper
1 teaspoon salt
¼ cup port wine

Place the minced shallot in a saucepan, add boiling water to cover, and simmer for 2 minutes. Drain and reserve. Put the orange and lemon zest in the same pan, add boiling water to cover, and simmer for 5 minutes, covered. Drain and reserve.

Remove the pits from the canned plums and chop coarse. Reserve the juice for another use. In a medium-sized, heavy-bottomed saucepan, combine all of the remaining ingredients, except the port wine. Heat to boiling and simmer until thick, stirring often. This should take about 30 minutes.

Place in a clean, nonreactive container and let sit, refrigerated, overnight. Add the port wine the following day. If you wish, you may process in canning jars in a boiling-water bath. (See Index for Canning Basics.)

Yield: 1 quart

SWEET-AND-TART PICKLED CRANBERRIES

The tartness of the vinegar and the cranberries is offset by the sweetness of the sugar and the enhancement from the spices, resulting in a complementary contrast in flavors. Be sure to let the cranberries rest for at least 2 to 3 days before serving for maximum taste potential. Serve with turkey, duck, or pheasant.

> 3 cups malt vinegar
> Juice of 2 lemons
> 4 cups granulated sugar
> 1 cup light corn syrup
> ½ teaspoon ground clove
> ¼ teaspoon ground mace
> 1 teaspoon ground nutmeg
> 1 tablespoon ground cinnamon
> 2 12-ounce packages cranberries,
>   fresh or frozen, washed and
>   picked over

In a medium-sized, nonreactive saucepan combine the vinegar, lemon juice, sugar, corn syrup, and spices. Bring the mixture to a full, rolling boil over medium heat.

Add the cranberries, lower the heat, and cook very slowly for 10 to 12 minutes, until the skins have cracked and the mixture is slightly thick.

Remove to a nonreactive container and refrigerate for 2 to 3 days before serving.

Yield: 2 quarts

CUCUMBER RELISH

Serve this relish as a starter to cleanse the palate before dinner, on top of a salad, or with sandwiches or burgers. These crunchy cucumber slices are addicting and are wonderful for a picnic or outdoor barbecue.

16 cucumbers, washed
5 ripe tomatoes, peeled and seeded
2½ cups salad oil
½ cup walnut oil
2 cups white-wine vinegar
1 cup tarragon vinegar
2 tablespoons salt
2 tablespoons freshly ground black pepper
2 large red onions, sliced very thin

Using a fork, score the skins of the cucumbers lengthwise all the way around. Slice them paper thin, using a mandoline or a food processor fitted with a fine slicing blade. Julienne the tomatoes as fine as possible.

Mix together the salad oil, walnut oil, vinegars, salt, and pepper.

Combine the sliced cucumbers, tomatoes, and red onions. Add the oil-vinegar mixture and toss well. Refrigerate overnight in a nonreactive container before serving.

Yield: 2 quarts

MINIATURE MIX

Miniature squashes are common during the summertime and come in several different varieties. Look for them at the local farmers' market. Serve them on top of salads or with a buffet as an interesting alternative to celery or carrot sticks.

2 dozen mini squashes (baby
    pattypan, zucchini, etc.)
1 cup whole baby corn, peeled
½ cup pearl onions, frozen
1 cup mini carrots, frozen
2 cups white-wine vinegar
1 cup water
1 tablespoon salt
½ cup granulated sugar
½ teaspoon turmeric
½ teaspoon mustard seeds
½ teaspoon pickling spice
1 teaspoon celery seeds

Clean the mini squashes by removing their stems and washing them thoroughly in cold water.

Place the squashes and other vegetables in a nonreactive saucepan and add the vinegar, water, salt, sugar, and spices. Bring to a full, rolling boil over medium heat and remove. Cover the pot with a lid and let cool to room temperature.

Transfer the mixture to a nonreactive container and store in the refrigerator overnight before using. (Miniature Mix may be canned; see Index for Canning Basics.)

Yield: 1 quart

MUSTARD PICKLES

There must be as many recipes for mustard pickles as there are grandmas who make them, and no two are the same. This version combines crunchy cucumbers, tomatoes, cauliflower, and peppers in a thick mustard dressing.

4 cucumbers, peeled and sliced
  ½ inch thick
1 pint cherry tomatoes
1 head cauliflower, broken into
  florets
2 red bell peppers, cut into ¼-inch
  dice
2 green bell peppers, cut into
  ¼-inch dice
2 cups salt
2 gallons water
1½ cups granulated sugar
1 tablespoon turmeric
½ cup all-purpose flour
½ cup salad-style mustard
2 tablespoons celery salt
1 tablespoon pickling spice
½ cup water

Place all the vegetables in a large bowl. Dissolve 1 cup of the salt in 1 gallon of the water and pour over the vegetables. Let sit overnight in the refrigerator.

Drain the vegetables and rinse thoroughly. Set aside.

Combine the remaining ingredients in a large, nonreactive saucepan and cook slowly over medium heat until thick, stirring constantly, for 15 to 20 minutes. The mixture should be thick enough to coat the back of a spoon.

Add the vegetables to the thickened brine and simmer for 15 minutes. Remove from the heat, cover, and let cool to room temperature. Store in a nonreactive container overnight before using. (Mustard Pickles may be canned; see Index for Canning Basics.)

Yield: 1 quart

PETER'S PICKLED PEPPERS

I actually got this recipe from a colleague named Peter Weiss, so I thought it was appropriate to name it after him. If you have a peck of peppers to pickle, this is certainly the recipe to use. I don't know what purpose the baking soda serves, other than perhaps to neutralize the acid from the peppers and in the brine. Serve these peppers in salads and sandwiches and with burgers, sausages, and hot dogs.

These should be made 2 days ahead of time.

6 green bell peppers
6 red bell peppers
6 yellow bell peppers
4 cups water
2 cups cider vinegar
2 teaspoons pickling spice
3 tablespoons granulated sugar
1 clove garlic, crushed
1 tablespoon salt
$\frac{1}{2}$ teaspoon baking soda

Hold the peppers on a cooking fork directly over an open gas flame and rotate slowly until the skins are completely charred. If you don't have a gas stove, place the peppers under the broiler and turn to char evenly on all sides.

Put all the charred peppers in a paper bag and seal well. The steam will loosen the skins. When cool, remove the peppers from the bag and scrape off their skins.

Cut the peppers in half and remove the seeds and cores. Set them aside in a nonreactive container. Make the pickling solution by combining the water, vinegar, pickling spice, sugar, garlic, and salt in a medium-sized, nonreactive saucepan. Bring this mixture to a full boil, then reduce the heat to simmer the mixture for 10 to 15 minutes. Then add the baking soda.

Pour the solution over the reserved peppers and let cool to room temperature. Cover tightly with plastic wrap and refrigerate for 2 days before using. (These pickled peppers may be canned; see Index for Canning Basics.)

Yield: Approximately 1½ quarts

ROOT-VEGETABLE RELISH MIX

Root vegetables, the heartiest of all vegetables, are combined here with fragrant herbs, vinegar, and oil. Not only is this relish delicious and easy to make, it also makes a colorful addition to any salad.

> 2 medium parsnips
> 2 large carrots
> 1 medium rutabaga
> 2 medium sweet potatoes
> 2 medium celery roots
> 2 medium turnips
> 3 large beets
> 1 cup Garlic-Herb Vinegar
>   Dressing (see Index)
> Salt and freshly ground black
>   pepper to taste

Place two medium-sized saucepans filled with water on the stove and bring the water in one to a full, rolling boil.

Peel and julienne the vegetables as thinly and uniformly as possible. Be sure to keep all the vegetables separate.

Prepare an ice-water bath using plenty of ice and cold water. Plunge the julienned parsnips, carrots, and rutabaga into one of the pans and simmer uncovered for 12 to 14 minutes. Add the sweet potatoes and simmer for another 5 to 7 minutes. Add the celery roots and turnips and cook for 12 more minutes. Drain immediately and plunge into the ice-water bath. Remove and drain well.

Bring the water in the other pot to a full, rolling boil, add the julienned beets, and simmer until tender but not mushy, about 9 to 10 minutes. Rinse under cold water and drain well. Add the beets to the other vegetables and toss in the Garlic-Herb Vinegar Dressing. Season to taste with salt and pepper. Refrigerate overnight before using.

Yield: 1 quart

ROASTED RED PEPPER–CORN RELISH

Back in the good old days, the wives of corn farmers often made corn relish from excess crops after a great harvest. They then sold the relish during the winter for extra income. This traditional recipe can be served as a starter, a side dish, or as part of a salad. Or in keeping with tradition, can it and give it to your friends and family at Christmastime. It should be made 2 days in advance of serving.

> 2 tablespoons unsalted butter
> 2 medium red onions, diced fine
> 2 medium stalks celery, diced fine
> 2 cups roasted, peeled, seeded,
>   and diced red bell pepper (see
>   Note)
> 2 tablespoons finely chopped
>   garlic
> 6 cups golden corn kernels, fresh
>   or canned
> 2 tablespoons dry English
>   mustard
> 1½ teaspoons turmeric
> 1 tablespoon celery seeds
> ½ teaspoon Tabasco
> 1 tablespoon Worcestershire sauce
> 2½ cups cider vinegar
> ¾ cup water

Heat the butter in a large, heavy, nonreactive saucepan. Add the onion, celery, pepper, garlic, and corn and cook covered over medium heat for 6 to 8 minutes. Add the spices, stir well, and cook covered for 5 more minutes. Add the remaining ingredients and bring the mixture to a boil over medium heat.

Lower the heat and simmer covered for 35 to 40 minutes until slightly thick, stirring occasionally.

Remove to a nonreactive container and store in the refrigerator at least 2 to 3 days before using. (Roasted Red Pepper-Corn Relish may be canned; see Index for Canning Basics.)

Note: See Peter's Pickled Peppers in Index for instructions on roasting and peeling peppers.

Yield: 1½ quarts

THREE-BERRY RELISH

This thick relish pairs well with smoked turkey, smoked duck, and ham. You might try variations using different berries from those listed. Always refrigerate this relish 24 hours or more before using it.

¾ cup fresh blueberries
¾ cup fresh blackberries
¾ cup fresh red currants
½ cup raisins
1 tablespoon finely chopped red
   onion
½ cup raspberry preserves
⅓ cup granulated sugar
1 teaspoon salt
¼ teaspoon cayenne pepper
¼ teaspoon ground ginger
Juice of ½ lemon

Pick over the fresh berries, discarding the stems. Wash well. (If these berries are not available fresh, try other varieties, or use frozen berries.)

Soak the raisins in water to cover for 1 hour. Drain well and reserve. Combine all the ingredients in a medium-sized saucepan. Bring the mixture to a boil; then reduce to a simmer. Simmer for 15 to 20 minutes, until the liquid thickens slightly.

Remove from heat and place in a nonreactive container. Refrigerate overnight before using.

Yield: 1 quart

ENTREES

Entrees are the main course—and the main reason many diners come to a particular restaurant. This is also the course that many chefs concentrate on, feeling that it gives them a chance to show what they can do.

The entrees at Prairie certainly reflect this attitude. Here you'll find many traditional meats and fish in new and exciting variations on old recipes. There's a burgoo made with buffalo and rabbit sausage, a roast chicken with the cornbread stuffing cooked outside the bird, and a Great Lakes whitefish with a tomato stew. Lots of wonderful ideas, and lots of terrific tastes and textures, using only the best the Midwest has to offer.

ROAST CHICKEN WITH CORNBREAD STUFFING AND CHIVE CREAM GRAVY

Makes a great meal served with a simple green salad.

1 to 2 tablespoons vegetable oil or
  unsalted butter
3 3-pound chickens, split in half,
  giblets reserved
1 tablespoon Hungarian paprika
Salt and freshly ground white
  pepper to taste

STUFFING
¼ pound chopped bacon
¼ cup diced celery
¼ cup diced onion
¼ cup diced button mushrooms
1 clove garlic, chopped fine
1 tablespoon chopped fresh
  parsley
¾ cup yellow cornmeal
¼ cup all-purpose flour
1 teaspoon baking powder
½ tablespoon granulated sugar
¼ teaspoon salt
1 egg, beaten
½ cup buttermilk
4 tablespoons (½ stick) unsalted
  butter, melted
½ cup canned corn kernels
½ teaspoon fresh sage
1 teaspoon fresh rosemary
Pinch salt
Pinch freshly ground white pepper

Continued on next page

GRAVY

1 shallot, peeled and diced fine
Reserved chicken giblets, diced
    fine
2 tablespoons diced onion
1 tablespoon unsalted butter
¼ cup dry white wine
1 leaf fresh sage
4 tablespoons chopped fresh
    chives
1 bay leaf
¼ teaspoon freshly cracked black
    pepper
¼ cup brown chicken gravy
¼ cup heavy cream
Salt and freshly ground white
    pepper to taste

GARNISH

6 tablespoons finely chopped fresh
    chives

Preheat the oven to 350°F. Heat the oil or butter in a large cast-iron skillet. Lightly sprinkle the chicken halves with paprika, and salt and pepper to taste.

Add the chicken halves to the skillet, one by one, browning them thoroughly on both sides before removing them. Place the chicken in a shallow roasting pan and roast in the preheated oven for about 40 minutes, or until golden brown.

To make the stuffing, preheat the oven to 375°F and butter a casserole dish. Cook the bacon until all fat is rendered. Reserve the bacon and strain the fat into a saucepan or skillet. Heat the fat in the pan, add the celery, onion, mushrooms, garlic, and parsley, and sauté until tender. Remove and drain well on paper towels.

Mix the cornmeal, flour, baking powder, sugar, and salt in a mixing bowl. Set aside. Combine the egg, buttermilk, melted butter, and the sautéed cooled vegetables. Stir in the reserved dry ingredients quickly, using as few strokes to mix as possible but being sure all ingredients are well mixed. Fold in the corn, the reserved bacon, sage, rosemary, salt, and pepper. Pour into the buttered casserole dish. Bake in the preheated oven for about 35 minutes, or until golden brown on the outside but moist inside. Cool and crumble slightly.

To make the gravy, combine the shallot, giblets, and onion in a saucepan and sauté in the butter over high heat until well browned. Add the white wine, sage, chives, bay leaf, and black pepper. Reduce the liquid slowly over medium heat until almost dry. Add the brown chicken gravy and reduce until thick, stirring constantly to avoid scorching. Add the cream and reduce over medium heat for about 5 minutes. Season to taste with salt and white pepper and strain through a fine strainer or cheesecloth.

To assemble: Serve each chicken piece on a heaping spoonful of gravy, put some of the stuffing on the side, and sprinkle generously with the chopped chives.

Yield: 6 servings

GRILLED HONEY-MUSTARD CHICKEN

This recipe should be started a day ahead. Serve with a good chardonnay or sauvignon blanc.

2 3-pound chickens, quartered, skin on

MARINADE
¼ cup walnut oil
1 12-ounce bottle catsup
½ cup honey
¼ cup vegetable oil
5 shallots, peeled and chopped fine
5 cloves garlic, peeled and chopped fine
¼ cup Dijon-style mustard
1 tablespoon dried tarragon
2 cups water

SAUCE
Reserved marinade
½ cup heavy cream
2 cups (4 sticks) unsalted butter, cut into 1-inch chunks
2 sprigs fresh tarragon, stemmed and chopped fine
Salt and freshly ground white pepper to taste

GARNISH
8 tablespoons chopped fresh chives (2 tablespoons per serving)

Bone the leg and thigh portions of the chicken. Combine all the ingredients for the marinade and blend thoroughly. Marinate the chicken for at least 24 hours in the refrigerator. Turn occasionally to be sure all the chicken is covered.

Light the grill. Remove the chicken from the marinade and place skin side down on the grill. Reserve the marinade for the sauce. Cook until the skin is crispy. Turn and continue to grill until the chicken is done. (On a moderately hot grill, this should take a total of 20 to 25 minutes.) Chicken can be cooked under the broiler as well.

While the chicken grills, prepare the sauce. Combine the reserved marinade and the cream in a nonreactive, medium-sized saucepan and over medium heat reduce slowly by half, or until thick enough to coat the back of a spoon. Slowly incorporate the butter, bit by bit, using a wire whisk, until it forms a good emulsion. Be careful that the sauce simmers and does not boil. Put the sauce in a blender and blend on high speed for 2 to 3 minutes, until smooth and silky. Strain the sauce through a fine sieve or cheesecloth and add the tarragon, salt, and pepper. Reserve in a warm place. After incorporating the butter, do not let the sauce boil or it will "break"— that is, appear grainy and greasy. Serve chicken sliced or whole atop the sauce and sprinkle with freshly chopped chives. To add extra flavor to the chicken, try grilling over wood: mesquite, hickory, or apple.

Yield: 4 servings

KANSAS CITY STRIP STEAKS WITH
HERBED MAYTAG BLUE CHEESE SAUCE

Serve with a good cabernet sauvignon, accompanied by Creamy Mashed Potatoes or Garlic and Parsley Potato Cakes (see Index).

¼ pound sliced bacon, julienned
4 bone-in strip steaks (about 1 pound each)
Salt and freshly ground black pepper to taste
2 shallots, peeled and chopped fine
2 cloves garlic, chopped fine
½ cup brandy
½ cup Madeira wine
1 cup Reduced Veal Stock (see Index)
1 cup heavy cream
1 sprig fresh rosemary, stemmed and chopped fine
2 sprigs fresh tarragon, stemmed and chopped fine
2 sprigs fresh thyme, stemmed and chopped fine
3 tablespoons chopped fresh chives
1 cup crumbled Maytag blue cheese
2 scallions, chopped fine

Preheat the oven to 350°F.

Put the bacon in a large cast-iron skillet and cook over medium heat until all the fat has been rendered and the bacon is crisp. Using a slotted spoon, remove the bacon and set it aside.

Season the steaks with salt and pepper. Add them, two at a time, to the skillet and sear them quickly on both sides over high heat until browned. Remove them from the skillet and repeat with the remaining steaks.

Return the steaks to the skillet and bake in the preheated oven for 10 to 12 minutes, until medium rare. Remove the steaks and set aside, keeping them warm. Add the shallots and garlic to the skillet and sauté for 5 minutes over medium heat. Pour off any excess fat from the skillet and carefully add the brandy. Cautiously ignite the brandy and let the flames die out naturally.

Add the Madeira and reduce until almost dry while scraping the bottom of the skillet with a wooden spoon. Add the veal stock and the cream and reduce slowly over medium heat by half. Stir in the herbs and blue cheese. Whisk well.

Ladle the sauce onto a serving platter and arrange the steaks over the top. Sprinkle the reserved bacon and scallions over all and serve immediately.

Yield: 4 servings

PRAIRIE BUFFALO BURGOO

This recipe probably originated on the old merchant ships sailing from Europe to the eastern coast of America. It eventually moved westward into the Midwest. The recipe I found called for buffalo and rabbit in a heavy bland sauce. I changed the recipe to include buffalo meat and rabbit sausage marinated in beer and wine for extra flavor. This recipe should be started a day in advance.

1 12-ounce can beer
½ cup dry red wine
2 pounds buffalo stew meat, cut into ¾-inch chunks
1 cup (2 sticks) unsalted butter
1 cup all-purpose flour
6 tablespoons vegetable oil
1 medium onion, chopped fine
2 pounds mushrooms, cleaned and quartered
1 bay leaf
1 teaspoon dried marjoram
2 leaves fresh sage
3 cups Reduced Veal Stock (see Index)
1 pound rabbit sausage (see Note)
3 carrots, peeled and diced fine
½ cup frozen pearl onions
Salt to taste
Freshly ground black pepper to taste

DOUGH

3 cups all-purpose flour
1½ teaspoons baking powder
1 teaspoon salt
2 eggs, beaten
¼ pound lard, softened
1 tablespoon sherry
4 tablespoons cold water
2 eggs, beaten

Preheat the oven to 350°F. Combine the beer and wine and marinate the buffalo meat overnight in the refrigerator.

In a microwave oven or a small saucepan, melt the butter. Add the flour and mix well. Place in an ovenproof dish and bake in the preheated oven for 30 minutes. Remove and let cool overnight.

The next day, strain off the liquid from the buffalo meat and reserve it for the sauce. Preheat the oven to 350°F. Heat the oil in a large saucepan and add the buffalo meat and the diced onion. Sauté over high heat until well browned. Remove with a slotted spoon and drain well. Set aside. Using the same pan, add the mushrooms and sauté until well browned. Remove with a slotted spoon and drain well. Set aside. Drain off any excess fat.

To the same pan add the reserved beer-wine marinade. Bring to a boil and reduce by one-third. Add the reserved buffalo-onion mixture and bring to a simmer. Add the bay leaf, marjoram, and sage. Add the reduced veal stock. Simmer for 1½ hours, until the meat is tender.

In the meantime, roll the rabbit sausage into 1-inch meatballs. Arrange on a cookie sheet and bake in the preheated oven for 30 minutes until done. Remove and set aside.

Add the reserved butter-flour mixture to the stew and stir well to dissolve. Add the reserved mushrooms, rabbit-sausage meatballs, carrots, and pearl onions. Simmer for 30 minutes, stirring frequently to prevent the stew from lumping or sticking to the bottom of the pot. Season to taste with salt and pepper. Set aside, keeping hot, and prepare the dough.

Continued on next page

In the bowl of an electric mixer fixed with a dough hook, sift together 2 cups of the flour, the baking powder, and the salt. Form a well in the center and add 2 eggs, the softened lard, sherry, and 2 tablespoons of water. Mix on low speed to form a wet mass. Add enough of the remaining flour to form a smooth, soft dough.

Remove from the bowl and let rest for 15 minutes. Roll the dough out to a thickness of ¼ inch and cut six circles approximately ½ inch larger than the diameter of six ovenproof soup bowls.

Put the reserved buffalo burgoo in the soup bowls. Cover each with a circle of dough, pressing the sides to form a good seal.

Combine the remaining 2 tablespoons of water with the 2 beaten eggs and generously brush the tops of the dough. Bake in the preheated oven for 20 to 25 minutes, until the dough has puffed and is well browned. Serve immediately.

Note: Rabbit sausage is available through Wild Game, Inc. (see Sources for Midwest Specialties).

Yield: 6 servings

STUFFED SHOULDER OF VEAL WITH APPLES, CHESTNUTS, AND CRANBERRIES

You may substitute pork shoulder if you like.

¼ pound bacon, diced fine
1 rib celery, diced fine
1 medium onion, peeled and
    chopped fine
2 Granny Smith apples, peeled,
    cored, and diced fine
1 cup finely chopped fresh
    mushrooms
½ cup canned chestnuts, slightly
    broken
½ cup cranberries
¼ cup apple wine
½ teaspoon salt
¼ teaspoon celery salt
⅛ teaspoon ground nutmeg
½ teaspoon fresh sage, chopped
    fine
1½ cups fresh bread crumbs
1 5-pound boneless veal shoulder
    roast
Salt to taste
Freshly ground white pepper to
    taste

SAUCE
2 shallots, peeled and chopped
    fine
1 cup apple cider
¼ cup Apple Butter (see Index)
1 tablespoon red-wine vinegar

Continued on next page

2 tablespoons lemon juice
3½ cups Reduced Veal Stock (see Index)
1½ cups heavy cream
1 cup (2 sticks) unsalted butter, cut into 1-inch cubes

GARNISH
3 Granny Smith apples, peeled, cored, and julienned
½ cup cranberries, blanched
½ cup canned whole chestnuts

Preheat the oven to 425°F.

Put the bacon in a large cast-iron skillet and cook over medium heat until all the fat is rendered and the bacon is crisp. Using a slotted spoon, remove the bacon and set it aside.

Add the celery and onion to the skillet and sauté for about 5 minutes, until the onion becomes transparent but not brown. Add the apples, mushrooms, chestnuts, and cranberries and cook, covered, for 15 to 20 minutes, or until the apples are tender.

In a large bowl combine the apple-mushroom mixture, reserved bacon, apple wine, salt, celery salt, nutmeg, sage, and bread crumbs. Mix well.

Stuff the cavity of the veal roast with the stuffing and tie securely with butcher's twine so that the stuffing will not come out. Season the meat with salt and ground white pepper. Place the meat on a roasting rack and roast on the center rack of the preheated oven, uncovered, for 30 minutes. Reduce the heat to 350°F and cook for 2 hours more, basting occasionally with the pan juices.

Remove the roast from the pan and set aside, keeping it warm. Pour off any excess fat and place the roasting pan on top of the stove. Add the shallots, apple cider, apple butter, vinegar, and lemon juice.

Let the mixture reduce until almost dry over medium heat, scraping the bottom of the pan occasionally with a wooden spoon. Add the reduced veal stock and the cream and simmer slowly for 15 to 20 minutes, until reduced by one-third.

Slowly incorporate the butter, whisking well after each addition, while keeping the sauce simmering but not boiling. Once all the butter is incorporated, pass the sauce through a fine sieve or a double layer of cheesecloth. Season with salt and white pepper. Slice the veal and ladle the sauce on top. Garnish with the julienned apples, cranberries, and chestnuts.

Yield: 8 to 10 servings

ROASTED RACK OF LAMB WITH PIMIENTO, GARLIC, AND ROSEMARY

The tanginess of the pimientos and mustard works well with the aromatic cilantro and the richness of the lamb. Ask your butcher for the lamb racks *Frenched* (which means that the rib bones are exposed). Serve with a nice California or Oregon Pinot Noir.

3 shallots, peeled
3 cloves garlic, peeled
3 sprigs fresh rosemary, stemmed
    and chopped
3 tablespoons finely chopped fresh
    cilantro
3 tablespoons finely chopped fresh
    parsley
5 pimientos, drained well
2 tablespoons salad-style mustard
½ cup (1 stick) unsalted butter
1 cup fine, dry bread crumbs
Salt and freshly ground black
    pepper to taste
2 lamb racks, Frenched, no fat
    cap, 4 bones each

In a food processor fitted with a steel blade, combine the shallots, garlic, rosemary, cilantro, parsley, and pimientos. Process for approximately 1 minute, until smooth.

Transfer the mixture to a small saucepan and simmer over medium heat until all the liquid has been evaporated and the mixture is dry. Let the mixture cool and transfer it back to the food processor. Add the mustard and butter and process the mixture to a smooth paste. Add the bread crumbs and process just until well mixed. Season well with salt and pepper. Remove and chill well for 2 to 3 hours before using.

Preheat the oven to 375°F. In the meantime, heat a cast-iron skillet over medium heat. Without adding any fat, place the racks top side down in the skillet and reduce the heat to low. Slowly brown the racks for 20 to 25 minutes, until they are well browned and have rendered a good amount of fat. Remove and drain; let them cool.

Gently pat the butter paste on the top side of the racks to form a nice, even, layered crust. Place the racks in a roasting pan in the preheated oven and cook for 20 to 30 minutes, until they are medium rare.

Remove the racks and let them rest for 15 minutes before slicing. To serve, slice the racks between the bones, making eight chops. Arrange the chops on a serving platter and serve immediately.

Yield: 2 servings

GRILLED PORK CHOPS WITH
BARBECUE BUTTER

Great for the barbecue and even better with an ice-cold midwestern beer such as Augsburger, Leinenkugel, or Christian Moerlin. This recipe should be started a day ahead.

> 2 cups (4 sticks) unsalted butter, softened
> ½ medium onion, chopped fine
> ½ cup Homemade Barbecue Sauce (see Index)
> ½ teaspoon cayenne pepper
> 1 tablespoon Hungarian paprika
> ¼ tablespoon salt
> 6 boneless, center-cut loin pork chops, 1½ inches thick
> Salt to taste
> Freshly ground black pepper to taste

Heat a small sauté pan over medium heat and add 1 tablespoon of the butter. Add the onion and sauté until it becomes transparent but not brown, about 6 to 8 minutes. Remove and set aside to cool.

Place the rest of the butter in the bowl of an electric mixer or a food processor fitted with a metal blade and whip on high speed for 8 to 10 minutes, until light and fluffy.

Add the reserved onion, barbecue sauce, cayenne pepper, paprika, and ¼ tablespoon salt. Mix until well blended.

Lay out a 10-inch piece of plastic wrap on a flat surface. Mound the butter evenly along the edge of the wrap closest to you. Roll the butter up in the plastic wrap tightly to form a long cylinder. Tie the ends of the plastic wrap and puncture the wrap in a couple of places to release any air bubbles.

Wrap the cylinder in another layer of plastic wrap and finally in aluminum foil. Freeze overnight before using.

Season the pork chops with salt and pepper and, preferably, grill them over hickory chips that have been soaked in water (or cook them under the broiler in the stove). Because of the size and cut of the chop it takes quite a while for the chops to cook through—about 20 minutes. If they brown too quickly, simply wrap them in foil and put them in a 350°F oven until they are cooked through (a meat thermometer inserted in the middle should read 160°F).

Arrange the chops on an ovenproof serving platter. Remove the barbecue butter from the freezer and remove the wrapping. Slice into circles about ¼ inch thick and place 1 circle of butter on top of each pork chop. Place under the broiler for approximately 30 seconds so that the butter melts slightly but not completely. Serve immediately.

Yield: 6 servings

PEPPER-CRUSTED VENISON STEAKS IN A BLACKBERRY GLAZE

Venison is prepared here in a cracked peppercorn crust and served with a rich sauce flavored with blackberries and port wine, offset by a dash of vinegar and tender herbs. This is sure to be a hit with game lovers. Since this is a rich and very flavorful dish, it should be served with a robust cabernet sauvignon.

GLAZE
½ cup fresh blackberries
2 shallots, peeled and chopped
    fine
¼ cup ruby port wine
Juice of 1 large orange
2 tablespoons blackberry preserves
6 tablespoons red-wine vinegar
¼ teaspoon cayenne pepper
2 sprigs fresh thyme
2 sprigs fresh tarragon
½ tablespoon whole black
    peppercorns
2 cups Reduced Veal Stock (see
    Index)
2 tablespoons unsalted butter
Salt and freshly ground black
    pepper to taste

STEAKS
4 tablespoons freshly cracked,
    coarsely ground black
    peppercorns
8 1-inch-thick boneless venison
    loin steaks (about 3 pounds)
3 tablespoons unsalted butter
½ cup red wine
8 to 10 blackberries
2 tablespoons chopped fresh
    chives

To make the glaze, in a medium saucepan combine the blackberries, shallots, port wine, orange juice, blackberry preserves, vinegar, cayenne, thyme, tarragon, and peppercorns. Bring to a boil over medium heat and reduce until there is about ¼ inch of liquid left on the bottom of the pan or until the mixture is thick and syrupy.

Add the reduced veal stock and whisk well to combine all the ingredients. Simmer 8 to 10 minutes longer and whisk in the 2 tablespoons of butter. Pass the sauce through a fine sieve or double layer of cheesecloth and season with salt and freshly ground black pepper. Set the sauce aside, keeping it warm.

Place the crushed pepper in a large bowl and add the venison steaks. Toss the steaks in the pepper, pressing it into the meat. Heat the 3 tablespoons of butter in a medium sauté pan or cast-iron skillet and add the steaks. Sauté 4 to 6 minutes on each side, until well browned and medium rare inside. Remove the steaks to a serving platter and keep them warm.

Pour any excess fat from the pan and deglaze it with the red wine, scraping the bottom with a wooden spoon to loosen the drippings. Let the wine reduce in the pan until almost dry. Add the reduced wine to the reserved sauce and mix well.

Pour the sauce over the reserved vension steaks. Garnish with the blackberries and chopped chives. Serve immediately.

Yield: 8 servings

PAN-ROASTED DUCK BREAST WITH
DRIED CHERRY AND PORT WINE SAUCE

I tried duck at several restaurants in Wisconsin and noticed that the dishes all had one thing in common: the duck was well done, dried out, and served in a cloying cherry sauce. Determined to change this midwestern concept of what we call "duck," I created what has turned out to be one of our signature dishes. It combines a dark, intense port wine sauce with tart dried Montmorency cherries from Michigan. (See Sources for Midwest Specialties for information about ordering the duck breast and dried cherries.) Follow the directions for cooking the breasts carefully because we have perfected a method that leaves the skin crispy and the meat pink and juicy without being fatty.

SAUCE
5 shallots, peeled and chopped
   fine
1 tablespoon cherry preserves
2 cups ruby port wine
2 tablespoons red-wine vinegar
2 bay leaves
1 tablespoon whole black
   peppercorns
4 sprigs fresh thyme
1 quart Reduced Veal Stock (see
   Index)
½ cup (1 stick) unsalted butter,
   cut into 1-inch chunks
Salt and freshly ground white
   pepper to taste

4 12-ounce baby duck breasts
5 tablespoons dried cherries (see
   Note)
4 tablespoons chopped fresh
   chives

To prepare the sauce, combine the shallots, preserves, port, vinegar, bay leaves, peppercorns, and thyme in a medium-sized, nonreactive saucepan. Reduce slowly over a medium flame until you have a thick syrupy glaze, approximately 20 to 25 minutes.

Add the reduced veal stock, and reduce again by about half. Add the butter, whipping in each piece until well incorporated before adding another. Season to taste and do not allow to boil again. Strain through a fine sieve or cheesecloth and reserve in a warm place.

Preheat the oven to 400°F.

To cook the duck, score the skin on the breasts in a crisscross pattern, making sure to score all the way down to the meat without cutting into it. Heat a sauté pan over high heat until very hot, and add the breasts skin side down. As soon as the fat starts to render, drain off the excess fat immediately and reduce the heat to medium-low. Return the pan to the heat and repeat the sautéing, always skin side down, for another minute or two, until the fat begins to accumulate. Drain off the excess fat again. (If you allow the fat to accumulate in the pan, the duck skin will boil in the fat instead of getting extra crispy.) Repeat this cycle of sautéing and draining another four or five times.

Turn the duck over and briefly sear the meat flesh side down for about 30 seconds. Now turn the meat skin side down again and place the sauté pan with the duck in it on the floor of the preheated oven. It should remain there for 6 minutes, or slightly less. Remove the meat from the oven and let it rest 6 to 8 minutes before slicing.

To assemble, use an electric knife to slice the breast, skin side up, into ¼-inch slices. Arrange the slices in a circular pattern on each plate. Gently ladle the sauce around the outside of the duck and add 5 or 6 dried cherries and the chopped chives.

Note: Dried cherries are available from American Spoon Foods (see Sources for Midwest Specialties).

Yield: 4 servings

COHO SALMON WITH BACON, LEEKS, AND BLACK WALNUTS

Coho salmon is also known as salmon trout and should be available at your local fish market. Black walnuts can be ordered from Dandy Pantry (see Sources for Midwest Specialties).

> 6 whole Coho salmon or brook
>   trout
> ¾ pound sliced bacon
> 1 leek
> 2 tablespoons unsalted butter
> 2 tablespoons Hungarian paprika
> Salt to taste
> Freshly ground black pepper to
>   taste
> 2 cups Lemon-Butter Sauce (see
>   Baked Stuffed Walleye Pike with
>   Four-Parsley Sauce in Index)
> 4 tablespoons black walnuts,
>   toasted (see Note)

Cut off the heads of the salmon or trout. Separate the fillets by cutting them down the middle with a sharp knife. Remove the back fins and carefully skin the 12 fillets. Set them aside.

Julienne the bacon as finely as possible and place in a medium-sized sauté pan. Place the pan over medium heat and cook the bacon until it is golden brown and crisp and all the fat has been rendered. Reserve the fat and drain the bacon well on paper towels.

Remove the root end of the leek and cut off the green top. Cut the leek in half and slice it as thinly as possible. Wash well under cold water and drain on a paper towel.

Melt the butter in a sauté pan over medium heat, add the leek, and cook until tender, approximately 10 to 12 minutes. Set aside.

Sprinkle the paprika evenly over the reserved fillets and season well with salt and pepper. Heat a cast-iron skillet over high heat and add the reserved bacon fat. Place the fillets skin side up in the skillet and cook over high heat for about 5 minutes. Flip the fillets over and cook for another 3 to 4 minutes.

Carefully remove the fillets from the pan and drain well. Arrange on a serving platter and ladle the Lemon-Butter Sauce over the top. Sprinkle with the reserved bacon, leek, and the black walnuts. Serve immediately.

Note: To toast walnuts, spread them out on a cookie sheet and bake in a preheated 325°F oven for 5 to 8 minutes.

Yield: 4 servings

GRILLED STURGEON WITH WOLLERSHEIM WINE SAUCE AND HORSERADISH

Sturgeon is native to the Midwest but is also farm-raised on the West Coast, thus making it available nationwide.

> 3 shallots, peeled and chopped fine
> 1 bay leaf
> 1 tablespoon black peppercorns
> ¼ cup sliced mushrooms
> 1 sprig fresh rosemary
> 3 cups Wollersheim Cul de Sac, or good zinfandel
> 2 cups heavy cream
> 2 pounds (8 sticks) unsalted butter, cut into 1-inch cubes
> Salt to taste
> Freshly ground black pepper to taste
> 4 8-ounce sturgeon fillets, pin bones out
> 4 tablespoons freshly grated horseradish
> 2 tablespoons chopped fresh chives

Combine the shallots, bay leaf, peppercorns, mushrooms, rosemary, and wine in a medium saucepan. Bring to a boil over medium heat and reduce until about ¼ inch of liquid is left in the bottom of the pan. Add the cream and bring to a boil. Whip well with a wire whisk. Reduce this mixture by half.

Slowly incorporate the butter, whisking well after each addition while keeping the sauce simmering but not boiling. Season with salt and freshly ground black pepper and strain through a fine sieve or a double layer of cheesecloth. Set the sauce aside, keeping it warm.

To cook the fish, rub the grill with some vegetable oil first to prevent the fish from sticking. Use regular charcoal with hickory or mesquite wood chips that have been soaked in water. Season the fish with salt and pepper and grill for 6 to 8 minutes on each side. Ladle some sauce on a serving platter and place the fish on top. Sprinkle with the fresh horseradish and chopped chives. Serve immediately.

Yield: 4 servings

BAKED STUFFED WALLEYE PIKE
WITH FOUR-PARSLEY SAUCE

You may substitute northern pike if walleye is not available.

> 10 8- to 10-ounce fillets walleye
>   pike (minimum 5 pounds total)
> 1 egg, beaten
> 2 cups heavy cream
> 4 tablespoons cooked barley
> 1 cup cooked wild rice
> ½ pound stemmed, blanched, and
>   drained spinach
> 2 carrots, peeled and diced
>   medium fine, parboiled
> 1 small red onion, chopped fine
>   and sautéed
> Salt and freshly ground white
>   pepper to taste
> Hungarian paprika
> ½ cup fish stock or dry white
>   wine
> 1 recipe Lemon-Butter Sauce
>   (recipe follows)
> 2 tablespoons chopped fresh
>   chervil
> 2 tablespoons chopped fresh curly
>   parsley
> 2 tablespoons chopped fresh
>   cilantro
> 2 tablespoons chopped fresh
>   broad-leaf parsley

Preheat the oven to 350°F. Pull the pin bones and skin from two of the pike fillets. Cut the fillets into medium-sized cubes. Chill thoroughly.

   Put the chilled, cubed fish in the bowl of a food processor fitted with a steel blade and puree until the fish is a very fine paste. Add the egg and continue to puree for about 45 seconds. Add the cream gradually until well incorporated, making sure not to overwhip and "break" the mousse, caus-

ing it to separate and become grainy. Stop the machine immediately as soon as all the cream has been added.

Fold in the barley, wild rice, spinach, carrots, and onion. Season to taste with salt and pepper. Set aside.

Trim the remaining fillets, skin them, and remove all the pin bones. Place one fillet in a baking dish or casserole, skin side down. Season lightly with salt and pepper. Put about one-fourth of the stuffing mixture on top. Top with another fillet, also skin side down, and sprinkle lightly with salt, pepper, and paprika. Make sure to use two fillets of the same size and place both skin side down with the tails lined up. Repeat with the remaining fillets and set aside.

Pour the fish stock or white wine carefully around the fillets. Bake in the preheated oven for 14 to 16 minutes or until done (thermometer will register 130°F). Be careful not to overcook. Remove from the pan and slice each stuffed fish into 8 to 10 ¼-inch slices with an electric knife. (Each stuffed fish makes two portions.) Arrange 4 or 5 slices on each plate and surround with about ¼ cup of Lemon-Butter Sauce. Sprinkle generously with the chopped four parsleys. Serve immediately.

Yield: 8 servings

Continued on next page

LEMON-BUTTER SAUCE

Juice of 4 lemons
½ cup dry white wine
1 teaspoon black peppercorns
1 bay leaf
2 shallots, peeled and diced fine
1 bunch fresh parsley, stems only
Splash white-wine vinegar
1½ cups heavy cream
1 pound (4 sticks) unsalted
    butter, cut into 1-inch cubes
Salt and freshly ground white
    pepper to taste

Combine the lemon juice, white wine, black peppercorns, bay leaf, shallots, parsley stems, and white-wine vinegar. Reduce over medium heat until almost dry. Add the heavy cream and reduce by two-thirds.

    Slowly incorporate the butter, piece by piece, while keeping the sauce at a good simmer. Make sure to whisk well with a wire whisk as each piece of butter is incorporated. It is important not to let the sauce boil once the butter has been incorporated or it will "break." Season to taste with salt and pepper and strain through a fine sieve. Serve immediately.

Yield: ½ quart

PLANKED LAKE SUPERIOR WHITEFISH
WITH WARM TOMATO STEW

Planking is the process of baking a piece of fish or meat on an oiled oak plank. Traditional planked whitefish is served on the plank on which it was baked, accompanied by whitefish livers and duchess potatoes.

> 4 red tomatoes
> 4 green tomatoes
> 4 yellow tomatoes
> ½ cup tomato juice
> 1 clove garlic, minced fine
> 2 sprigs fresh thyme
> 1 sprig fresh tarragon
> 6 leaves fresh basil, shredded fine
> Salt and freshly ground white
>   pepper to taste
> 4 whitefish fillets (about 2
>   pounds total), pin bones
>   removed
> 2 scallions, chopped fine

Fill a very large stockpot with water and bring to a full, rolling boil. Prepare an ice-water bath using plenty of ice and cold water.

Score the bottom of each tomato in a crisscross pattern and plunge them into the boiling water. Let the tomatoes sit in the hot water for only 1 minute. Remove immediately and plunge into the ice-water bath. When the tomatoes are cool enough to handle, gently peel off the skins and discard them. Remove the cores and slice each tomato in half. Scoop out the seeds and chop the tomatoes fine.

In a medium-sized, nonreactive saucepan combine the tomatoes, tomato juice, garlic, thyme, tarragon, and basil. Cook over low heat, covered, until the tomatoes render all their juices, about 20 minutes.

Continued on next page

125

Preheat the oven to 350°F. Remove the tomatoes from the heat and drain them in a strainer, carefully reserving all the juices. Return the juice to the heat and bring to a boil. Reduce the heat and let the juice reduce for about 20 minutes, or by half. Season well with salt and pepper. Set both the chopped tomatoes and the juice aside and keep warm.

Place the whitefish fillets skin side down on a well-oiled oak plank and roast in the oven until done, about 20 minutes. Remove and place the fillets on four separate plates. Top with the chopped tomatoes and tomato broth. Sprinkle with chopped scallions.

Yield: 4 servings

TRADITIONAL ROAST TURKEY WITH WHOLE-WHEAT SAGE STUFFING AND GIBLET GRAVY

This traditional favorite is given a new twist by replacing the standard dry, bland, white-bread stuffing with a flavorful whole-wheat stuffing infused with fresh sage. Notice that the stuffing is made separately from the bird rather than stuffed inside it. It is not advisable to cook stuffing inside the cavity of any poultry because of the risk of food-borne bacteria.

1 10- to 12-pound fresh turkey
Salt to taste
Freshly ground black pepper to taste
1 cup (2 sticks) unsalted margarine, melted

STUFFING
½ pound whole-wheat bread
½ cup (1 stick) unsalted butter
1 medium onion, peeled and chopped fine
2 ribs celery, diced fine
¾ cup Basic Chicken Stock (see Index)
2 teaspoons fresh sage, chopped fine
¾ teaspoon dried thyme
⅛ teaspoon ground nutmeg
1 teaspoon poultry seasoning
½ teaspoon salt
½ teaspoon freshly ground black pepper

GRAVY
3 cups Basic Chicken Stock (see Index)
1 bay leaf

Continued on next page

1 clove
½ teaspoon whole black
    peppercorns
2 tablespoons cornstarch
4 tablespoons cold water
Reserved giblets
4 tablespoons (½ stick) unsalted
    butter
Salt to taste
Freshly ground black pepper to
    taste

Preheat the oven to 425°F.

Remove the giblets from the turkey and dice them fine. Set them aside. Rinse the turkey thoroughly under cold, running water and drain well on paper towels.

Season the turkey thoroughly inside and out with salt and freshly ground black pepper. Place on a rack in a roasting pan and rub well with the melted margarine. Place the turkey on the center rack of the preheated oven for 25 minutes and reduce the heat to 350°F. Continue to roast for approximately 4 hours (or until it registers 150°F on a meat thermometer inserted in the breast), basting frequently with the pan juices that have accumulated. While the turkey is roasting, prepare the stuffing.

Trim the crust off the bread and cut the bread into ½-inch cubes. Place the bread on a cookie sheet and place in the preheated 350°F oven. Cook for 12 to 14 minutes, until the edges begin to dry out but the cubes are still soft and fluffy if pressed between your fingers. Remove from the oven and set aside.

Melt the butter in a cast-iron skillet and add the onion and celery. Sauté the vegetables over medium heat for 8 to 10 minutes, until the onion becomes transparent. Add the reserved bread cubes and the chicken stock, herbs, salt, and pepper. Cook slowly over medium heat, stirring constantly with a wooden spoon, until all of the liquid has been absorbed and the mixture is well blended.

Butter a shallow, ovenproof dish. Transfer the mixture to the dish, cover, and bake for 30 minutes in the preheated oven. Remove and set aside, keeping it warm.

When the turkey is done, prepare the gravy by removing the turkey from the roasting pan and draining off as much fat as possible. Place the roasting pan on top of the stove and add the chicken stock. Bring to a boil over medium heat and add the bay leaf, clove, and peppercorns.

Reduce the heat to low and simmer, scraping the bottom of the pan vigorously with a wooden spoon to dissolve all the drippings from the turkey. Combine the cornstarch and water in a small bowl and whisk well to dissolve. Pour this mixture into the simmering chicken stock and whisk constantly for 3 to 5 minutes, until it is well dissolved and the gravy has thickened. Do not allow it to boil at this point.

Pass the gravy through a fine sieve or a double layer of cheesecloth into a saucepan. Place the pan over medium heat and bring the gravy back to a boil. Add the reserved giblets and simmer for 8 to 10 minutes. Whisk in the butter and season to taste with salt and pepper. Carve the turkey and serve hot with the stuffing and giblet gravy.

Yield: Approximately 8 servings

VEGETABLES AND SIDES

Perhaps nowhere does Prairie's dedication to regional tradition show up better than in vegetables and sides. In contrast to all the trendy new vegetables we've all had to get used to, Prairie goes back to the vegetables we remember from childhood. On the winter menu you'll find root vegetables and grains—dishes like Glazed Turnips and Pearl Barley Pilaf.

Fiddlehead ferns could only mean spring. Summer brings beloved favorites like corn on the cob, this time grilled with Prairie's own barbecue sauce. Late summer brings broccoli, wild rice, and the squashes. Prairie offers broccoli fritters, serves the wild rice in a casserole with mushrooms, and creams the butternut squash with honey and brown sugar. All good reasons to love your vegetables.

PEARL BARLEY PILAF

Serve this with any simple meat recipe as an interesting alternative to the more mundane white rice pilaf. As always, start with a rich and flavorful stock for the best results.

3½ cups Basic Chicken Stock (see
    Index)
½ cup dry white wine
4 tablespoons (½ stick) unsalted
    butter
¼ cup finely chopped onion
2 sprigs fresh thyme
1 bay leaf
2 cups pearl barley
½ teaspoon salt
¼ teaspoon freshly ground black
    pepper

Preheat the oven to 375°F.

Combine the chicken stock and wine in a medium-sized saucepan, and bring to a full, rolling boil. Melt 2 tablespoons of the butter in another medium-sized saucepan. Add the onion and sauté over medium heat for 5 to 7 minutes, until transparent but not brown. Add the thyme, bay leaf, and barley and cook, stirring constantly, 3 to 4 minutes longer.

Add the boiling chicken stock, salt, and pepper. Cover and bring this mixture to a boil, stirring occasionally. Place the covered saucepan in the preheated oven and cook for approximately 35 minutes, or until all the liquid has been absorbed and the barley is tender.

Remove and let stand, covered, for 15 minutes. Add the remaining butter and stir well. Serve hot.

Yield: 3 cups (6 servings)

BROCCOLI FRITTERS WITH
CHEDDAR HOLLANDAISE

Try substituting different vegetables such as cauliflower, zucchini, or sweet potatoes. Serve the fritters family style in the middle of the table, and let your guests help themselves to the sauce.

Oil for deep frying
2 pounds fresh broccoli

FRITTER BATTER
4 eggs, separated
1½ cups beer
4 tablespoons (½ stick) unsalted
    butter, melted
1 teaspoon baking powder
2 cups all-purpose flour
½ teaspoon salt
¼ teaspoon freshly ground white
    pepper
2 cups Cheddar Cheese
    Hollandaise (see Index)

Preheat a deep fryer or heavy pot of oil to 350°F.

Wash the broccoli and drain well. Pat dry with paper towels. Trim the broccoli into bite-size florets. Set aside.

In a bowl combine the egg yolks, beer, and melted butter. Mix well. Sift together the baking powder, flour, salt, and white pepper. Combine the wet ingredients with the dry and mix well to combine.

Whip the egg whites so that they hold medium-stiff peaks, and using a rubber spatula, gently fold them into the batter. Use immediately.

Drop the broccoli florets into the batter and coat each one generously. Deep-fry until golden brown. Drain well on paper toweling and serve hot with Cheddar Cheese Hollandaise.

Yield: Approximately 4 servings

DILLED BABY CARROTS

Although baby carrots are much more tender than the adults, it is possible to substitute peeled sliced adult carrots and even parsnips in this recipe. Try to use pickle juice if you have some, as it really brings out the flavor of the dill.

1½ pounds baby carrots, tops on
2 tablespoons unsalted butter
3 tablespoons chopped fresh dill
1 bay leaf, crushed
1 tablespoon pickle juice or white
    vinegar
Salt to taste
Freshly ground white pepper to
    taste

Peel the carrots and cut the tops, leaving ½ inch of stem. Fill a medium saucepan with water. Bring to a full, rolling boil. Add the carrots and cook over medium heat for 15 to 20 minutes, or until tender but not mushy.

Remove to a colander and drain well. Heat the butter in a medium-sized sauté pan. Add the chopped dill and the crushed bay leaf and mix well. Add the carrots and toss to coat them thoroughly.

Add the pickle juice or white vinegar and season with salt and pepper. Serve hot.

Yield: 4 servings

CELERY ROOT PUREE

If celery root is unavailable, try substituting other root vegetables such as carrots, turnips, rutabagas, or sweet potatoes. And if you happen to have any leftover broccoli stems (from the Broccoli Fritters, for example), use them to make a broccoli puree by simply replacing the celery root with an equal amount of broccoli.

2 pounds celery root
2 tablespoons unsalted butter
¼ teaspoon freshly grated nutmeg
½ cup heavy cream
Salt to taste
Freshly ground white pepper to
    taste

Using a paring knife, trim the celery root and cut off the tough outer skin. Cut into ½-inch chunks.

Fill a medium saucepan with water and bring to a full, rolling boil over medium heat. Add the celery root and simmer for 25 to 30 minutes, until soft. Drain well in a strainer or colander.

Transfer the still-warm celery root to a food processor fitted with a metal blade and puree until smooth and velvety. Return the puree to the saucepan and heat over low heat, stirring frequently. Add the butter, nutmeg, and cream. Season with salt and pepper and serve hot.

Yield: Approximately 4 servings

BARBECUED CORN ON THE COB

Try to find good, fresh, sweet corn. To check for freshness, pop a kernel on the cob and look for a milky white juice. As soon as the corn is off the stalk, its sugars immediately convert to starches, so try to buy it at a local farmers' market or roadside stand, where the person who sells it to you is probably the one who grew it and picked it fresh that morning.

6 ears fresh corn, in the husk
1 cup Homemade Barbecue Sauce
(see Index)

Soak the corn in plenty of water for at least 3 to 4 hours.

Prepare the grill. Grill the corn over the hot coals for 30 to 35 minutes. Husk the corn while still hot and baste generously with the barbecue sauce. Serve hot.

Yield: 6 servings

SWEET-AND-SOUR FIDDLEHEAD FERNS

Fiddleheads are so called because they curl up tightly and resemble the head of a fiddle or violin. They are generally available for about two or three weeks around the middle of May. Look for tightly curled ferns free of blemishes and insects.

4 cups fresh fiddlehead ferns
¼ pound bacon, julienned
3 tablespoons walnut oil
¼ cup raspberry vinegar
3 tablespoons honey
Salt to taste
Freshly ground black pepper to
      taste

Cut off all the brown, dry parts of the fiddleheads and rinse them well in cold water.

Fill a large stockpot with water and bring to a full, rolling boil. Prepare an ice-water bath using plenty of cold water and ice.

Plunge the fiddleheads into the boiling water and simmer, uncovered, for about 8 minutes, or until tender. Remove to the ice-water bath and let cool. Drain well in a colander.

In a large sauté pan, cook the bacon until it is golden brown and all the fat has been rendered. Let the fat cool slightly and add the walnut oil, vinegar, and honey.

Bring the mixture to a boil over medium heat and add the reserved fiddleheads. Toss the mixture until the fiddleheads are heated through. Season to taste with salt and pepper. Serve hot.

Yield: Approximately 6 servings

GARLIC AND PARSLEY POTATO CAKES

These crispy browned potato cakes flavored with sweet garlic and aromatic cilantro are a perfect accompaniment to Roasted Rack of Lamb, Pepper-Crusted Venison Steaks, or Pan-Roasted Duck Breast. The tricky part of the preparation is making sure that the potatoes are broken up by hand and left somewhat chunky in the mixture. Otherwise, the patties will become too moist and will fall apart when sautéed.

> 5 medium russet potatoes
> 2 eggs, beaten
> 1 tablespoon finely chopped fresh
>   parsley
> 2 tablespoons finely chopped fresh
>   cilantro
> 3 cloves garlic, chopped fine
> Salt to taste
> Freshly ground black pepper to
>   taste
> ¼ cup bacon fat or vegetable oil

Place the potatoes in a large saucepan and cover with water. Place on high heat and bring the water to a boil. Boil the potatoes for approximately 25 minutes, or until they are just tender enough to be easily pierced with a fork.

Remove and drain well in a colander. Let the potatoes cool. Using a paring knife, gently peel the skins off. Break the potatoes up into large chunks by hand and place them in a bowl. Add the eggs, parsley, cilantro, garlic, salt, and black pepper. Gently toss the mixture to incorporate all the ingredients evenly.

Divide the mixture into six equal portions. Form each into a patty about ¼ inch thick. Chill for at least 1 hour.

Heat a large cast-iron skillet over medium heat and add the bacon fat or vegetable oil. Add the patties and sauté over medium heat for 5 to 6 minutes, or until golden brown all over. Remove and drain well on paper towels. Serve immediately.

Yield: 6 cakes (6 servings)

STUFFED MOREL MUSHROOMS

Morel mushrooms are generally available in mid- to late spring and are also known as sponge mushrooms because they look and feel like tiny auburn-colored sponges. Look for mushrooms that are unblemished and firm to the touch. Since these mushrooms grow on the forest floor, it is not unusual for them to be covered with sand and dirt, so wash them well. For this recipe it is essential that you use *fresh* morels.

12 large, fresh morels
2 cups finely chopped button
    mushrooms
2 cups water
Juice of 1 lemon
3 tablespoons unsalted butter
Pinch salt
3 shallots, peeled and chopped
    fine
¾ cup fine, dry bread crumbs
3 tablespoons chopped fresh
    chives
1 tablespoon chopped fresh
    parsley
½ teaspoon celery salt
⅛ teaspoon ground nutmeg
⅛ teaspoon cayenne pepper
¼ cup Basic Chicken Stock (see
    Index)
Salt to taste
Freshly ground black pepper to
    taste
2 tablespoons walnut oil
1 cup morel puree (recipe follows)

MOREL PUREE
1 pound fresh morels, cleaned
4 shallots, peeled and minced
2 sprigs fresh thyme

2 sprigs fresh tarragon
¼ cup white wine
1 quart Basic Chicken Stock (see
   Index)
1 cup heavy cream

Wash the morels gently but thoroughly under cold, running water to remove all the sand and grit. Cut off the stems and set the morels aside. Chop the stems very fine and add them to the 2 cups of chopped mushrooms, which will be used for the filling.

Combine the water, lemon juice, 1 tablespoon of the butter, and the salt in a medium saucepan. Bring to a boil and add the morels. Simmer for 1 minute, and using a slotted spoon, carefully remove them. Let them drain well on paper towels while preparing the stuffing.

Heat the remaining 2 tablespoons of butter in a medium sauté pan and add the shallots and the chopped mushrooms. Sauté for 15 to 20 minutes, until the mushrooms are thoroughly cooked and the juices have evaporated. Add the bread crumbs, 1 tablespoon of the chopped chives, parsley, celery salt, nutmeg, cayenne pepper, and chicken stock. Mix well with a wooden spoon and cook over medium heat for 8 to 10 more minutes, until the mixture is smooth. Season with salt and freshly ground black pepper.

For the morel puree, sweat the morels, shallots, and fresh herbs in a medium-sized covered saucepan for 6 to 7 minutes. Add the white wine and reduce until almost dry. Add the chicken stock and reduce by half. Add the cream and puree very well in a blender or food processor until smooth and velvety.

Let the stuffing cool and then pipe it through a pastry bag fitted with a fine tube into the reserved morels. Heat the walnut oil in a medium sauté pan and add the morels. Sauté them slowly until they are heated through. Remove them to a serving platter and serve hot with the morel puree and the remaining chopped chives.

Yield: 4 servings

CREAMY MASHED POTATOES

The secret to great mashed potatoes is to keep them as hot as possible throughout the preparation.

2 pounds russet potatoes
8 tablespoons (1 stick) unsalted
   butter
1 cup half-and-half
1 teaspoon salt
½ teaspoon freshly ground white
   pepper
¼ teaspoon ground nutmeg

Peel the potatoes and place them in a large pot. Cover with water and bring to a full, rolling boil. Boil until the potatoes are very soft, about 1 hour. Remove and drain well in a colander.

In the meantime, combine the butter and half-and-half in a medium saucepan and bring to a boil. Mash the potatoes by putting them through a ricer, a meat grinder, or a sieve, or by mashing with a potato masher.

Return them to a clean, dry pan and place the pan over low heat. Gradually add the butter mixture while whisking continuously with a wire whisk. Add the salt, pepper, and nutmeg. Beat vigorously for 1 minute. Serve immediately.

Yield: 6 servings

CREAMED BUTTERNUT SQUASH
WITH HONEY AND BROWN SUGAR

Honey and dark brown sugar accentuate the flavor of the velvety butternut squash in this recipe. Serve with Traditional Roast Turkey, Pan-Roasted Duck Breast, or Prairie Buffalo Burgoo for rave reviews.

2 to 3 butternut squashes, about
    2½ pounds total
8 tablespoons (1 stick) unsalted
    butter, melted
¼ cup honey
¼ cup dark brown sugar, packed
¼ teaspoon ground cinnamon
⅛ teaspoon ground nutmeg
¼ cup heavy cream
Salt to taste
Freshly ground white pepper to
    taste

Preheat the oven to 350°F. Wash the squashes and drain well. Cut each squash in half lengthwise and scoop out the seeds and the stringy pulp. Arrange the squash cut side up in a baking dish.

Combine the butter, honey, brown sugar, cinnamon, and nutmeg in a bowl. Mix well. Pour the honey-butter mixture into the cavities of the squash, distributing it evenly.

Cover the dish with aluminum foil and place on the center rack of the preheated oven. Bake for 1¼ to 1½ hours, until the squash is soft and mushy. During the baking process, be sure to baste the squash occasionally with the accumulated pan juices. In the meantime, heat the cream in a small saucepan.

Remove the squash from the oven. When the squash is cool enough to handle, take a large spoon and scrape the flesh from the rind into the bowl of a food processor fitted with a steel blade. Add the pan juices and puree the squash just until smooth. (If processed too long it will become watery.)

Remove the mixture from the processor to a bowl and add the hot cream. Mix well and season to taste with salt and pepper. Serve hot.

Yield: Approximately 4 servings

BAKED TOMATO AND
WILD-MUSHROOM CUSTARD

Serve this as a side for such fish entrees as the Coho Salmon, Planked Lake Superior Whitefish, or Grilled Sturgeon. It may also be served on its own for a Sunday brunch buffet.

> 4 tablespoons (½ stick) unsalted
>   butter
> 1 medium onion, peeled and
>   chopped fine
> 2 cloves garlic, chopped fine
> 1 cup peeled, seeded, and finely
>   chopped tomato
> 2 sprigs fresh tarragon, stemmed
>   and chopped fine
> 1 cup sliced button mushrooms
> ½ cup sliced oyster mushrooms
> ½ cup white trumpet mushrooms
> Salt and freshly ground black
>   pepper to taste
> 9 eggs, beaten
> 1½ cups heavy cream
> ⅓ cup whole milk
> ½ teaspoon ground nutmeg
> 1 teaspoon salt

Preheat the oven to 350°F. Butter a 2-quart soufflé dish. Set aside.

Heat 2 tablespoons of the butter in a large sauté pan over medium heat. Add the onion and sauté for 6 to 8 minutes, until the onion is transparent but not brown. Add the garlic and tomato and cook for 5 minutes longer. Add the chopped tarragon and toss well to combine. Transfer the mixture to a large bowl and return the pan to the heat.

Heat the remaining 2 tablespoons of butter over high heat and add all of the mushrooms. Brown well over high heat until soft and combine with the tomato mixture. Season well with salt and pepper and transfer to the buttered soufflé dish.

Combine the eggs, cream, milk, nutmeg, and salt in a large bowl and whisk well using a wire whisk. Pour the egg mixture over the vegetables and gently mix with a wooden spoon to combine. Season with black pepper.

Place the dish on the middle rack of the preheated oven and bake until brown and puffy, approximately 1 hour. Remove and let the custard rest for approximately 1 hour before serving. Serve warm.

Yield: 6 servings

TOMATO ASPIC

An unusual but flavorful combination of tomatoes, herbs, and gelatin makes this an interesting garnish for smoked meats, a side dish for a buffet, or a centerpiece for a platter of crudités.

This recipe should be made a day ahead.

¼ cup cold water
2 tablespoons powdered gelatin
1½ cups tomato juice
1 tablespoon grated onion
1 teaspoon chopped fresh
    tarragon
½ teaspoon fresh thyme leaves
3 tomatoes, peeled, seeded, and
    chopped fine
1 tablespoon lemon juice
1 teaspoon granulated sugar
¼ teaspoon Tabasco
1 teaspoon Worcestershire sauce
½ teaspoon salt
¾ teaspoon freshly ground black
    pepper

Combine the water and the gelatin and let sit for 6 minutes. Set aside. Place the tomato juice in a medium saucepan and add the reserved gelatin mixture. Heat over low heat, stirring well, just until the gelatin has dissolved.

Add the remaining ingredients and stir well. Transfer to a nonreactive container. Place in the refrigerator and stir occasionally until set to insure that the ingredients don't settle to the bottom.

Chill well overnight. To unmold, briefly dip the container in a larger container of hot water. Invert onto a serving platter and slice. Serve immediately.

Yield: 2¼ cups (8 to 10 servings)

GLAZED TURNIPS

Try combining or replacing the turnips with other root vegetables such as carrots, parsnips, or rutabagas for more flavor and variety. This hearty side dish is great with stews and roasts.

8 medium turnips
2 tablespoons unsalted butter
2 tablespoons honey
½ teaspoon salt
⅛ teaspoon ground mace
2 tablespoons chopped fresh
    herbs—parsley, thyme,
    tarragon, coriander, and
    chives—combined
Salt to taste
Freshly ground white pepper to
    taste

Scrub the turnips thoroughly and cut them into ¼-inch wedges. Place in a medium saucepan with enough water to cover and bring to a boil. Simmer for approximately 15 minutes, until tender. Drain well.

Heat the butter, honey, salt, and mace in a large sauté pan or skillet. Place the turnips in the pan and shake the pan over medium heat, tossing until all the vegetables are well glazed and heated through.

Add the freshly chopped herbs and season to taste with salt and pepper. Serve immediately.

Yield: 4 servings

WILD RICE AND MUSHROOM CASSEROLE

This is a traditional side dish that combines wild rice, mushrooms, and barley in a savory beef broth. It's a winner when served with steaks, chops, roasts, or turkey.

1 cup (2 sticks) unsalted butter
1 medium onion, chopped fine
1¼ cups long-grain wild rice
2 tablespoons pearl barley
4 cups beef broth
4 sprigs fresh thyme
½ pound button mushrooms,
    cleaned and quartered
Salt to taste
Freshly ground black pepper
    to taste

Melt half the butter in a medium saucepan. Add the onion and sauté over medium heat for 6 to 8 minutes, until transparent but not brown.

Add the wild rice and barley and cook for another 5 minutes, until the rice is well coated with the butter. Add the beef broth and thyme and bring to a boil over high heat. Reduce the heat to a simmer and cook, covered, for approximately 1 hour, stirring occasionally. Remove from the heat and let stand, covered, for about 15 minutes, or until all the liquid has been absorbed.

Melt the remaining butter in a medium sauté pan over high heat. Add the mushrooms and brown well on all sides. Add the mushrooms and the pan juices to the wild rice. Stir well. Season to taste with salt and black pepper. Remove the thyme sprigs and serve hot.

Yield: 6 servings

COTTAGE CHEESE

A talented cheese maker from Wisconsin convinced me that the easiest cheese to make is cottage cheese and that once I learned to make it well I could flavor it any way I wanted. Ingredients such as lemon balm, chives, or roasted peppers—the possibilities are endless—can be added when the curd is heated.

> 1½ gallons whole milk
> 1 cup buttermilk
> 1 rennet tablet
> 1½ teaspoons salt
> ½ cup heavy cream
> ½ cup sour cream

Combine the milk and the buttermilk in a large bowl. Mix well and let sit for 2 to 3 hours, or until it reaches room temperature. Remove about ¼ cup of the milk-buttermilk mixture and heat until tepid. Add the rennet to the warmed milk and stir to dissolve.

Add the rennet mixture to the milk-buttermilk mixture and mix well. Let the mixture sit, covered, at room temperature until the curd has formed, about 14 to 16 hours.

In the top of a double boiler slowly heat the curd until just barely warm (no more than 115°F). Cook slowly while maintaining that barely warm temperature, stirring frequently so it will heat evenly throughout.

After 1½ hours remove the curd from the heat and gently strain through a double layer of cheesecloth. Let drain well for about 1 hour, or until the curd is dry. Discard the strained liquid (the whey).

Add the salt, heavy cream, and sour cream to the curd. Mix gently to combine the ingredients. Transfer to a glass, crockery, or plastic container and refrigerate.

Yield: 1 quart

▪ ▪ ▪
DESSERTS
▪ ▪ ▪

Dessert is highly regarded in the Midwest. This is pie country, a part of the world where baking pies is an important measure of a cook. Visit any church supper and you'll see the ranks of pies put out. The county and state fairs all over the Midwest award dozens of ribbons and cash prizes to the best pies each year. Read descriptions of food put out for haying and threshing crews and you will know what pie baking is all about. Those crews would time their work to be sure they ate well, ending their day on the fields of the farmer whose wife was the best cook. Any farm wife worth her salt would put at least three kinds of pie on the table for the noon dinner.

Prairie's menu reflects this heritage. We offer plenty of pies, some of which take advantage of seasonal midwestern fruits and all of which are firmly rooted in tradition. Prairie's menu has other dessert recipes that are adaptations of (and, we hope, improvements on) midwestern favorites, like the Warm Chocolate Pudding Cake with Marshmallow-Mint Whipped Cream or the Carrot Cake with Orange Glaze. There is an old-fashioned blackberry cobbler with a new twist—maple custard—and a persimmon pudding made with a sprinkle of dried blueberries, which is the restaurant's most popular dessert.

BASIC PIE DOUGH

The trick to making pie dough is twofold. First is the type of shortening used—you'll note that this recipe calls for equal amounts of lard and butter. The lard is for leavening—to make the dough flaky—while the butter is strictly for flavor. The second trick is: *don't overmix*. Mix the dough just until it comes together. If it is overmixed gluten will form in the flour and make the dough tough. This dough will need to be made in advance, as it must chill for 4 hours or overnight.

> 2 cups all-purpose flour
> 1 teaspoon salt
> ¼ pound lard and ¼ pound
>   (1 stick) unsalted butter,
>   mixed
> ½ cup granulated sugar
> 1 teaspoon white vinegar
> 1 egg, beaten
> Ice water as needed

Combine the flour and salt in a nonreactive mixing bowl. Cut the lard-butter mixture into the flour-salt mixture with a fork or a pastry blender just until the mixture resembles coarse meal. Do not overmix.

One by one, add the sugar, the vinegar, and the egg, tossing lightly with a fork after each addition. Sprinkle in ice water, tablespoon by tablespoon, gently tossing the loose particles around the bowl to absorb the moisture. Keep adding and tossing until the particles adhere to form a moist, but not wet, mass that will hold together without any dry or crumbly parts. Wrap and chill for a minimum of 4 hours or overnight before using.

Let stand at room temperature for 15 to 20 minutes before rolling out on a floured surface.

Yield: Enough dough for 1 two-crust pie

DAIRYLAND SOUR CREAM–RAISIN PIE

I traded one of my recipes for this one with Elli Mitchell, a grandmother of twelve who lives in Milwaukee.

1½ cups raisins
½ cup water
½ cup granulated sugar
½ cup dark brown sugar, packed
1 tablespoon all-purpose flour
¼ teaspoon salt
¼ teaspoon ground nutmeg
¼ teaspoon ground clove
¼ teaspoon ground cinnamon
⅓ cup lemon juice
1½ teaspoons lemon zest
3 eggs
1 cup sour cream
1 9-inch prepared pie shell
¼ pound (approximately) pie
   dough or scraps
1 tablespoon water
1 egg yolk

Preheat the oven to 450°F. Put the raisins and water in a small saucepan and bring to a boil. Reduce heat and simmer for about 5 minutes. Set aside. Mix together the sugar, brown sugar, flour, salt, nutmeg, clove, cinnamon, lemon juice, and lemon zest. Stir the dry mixture into the reserved raisin-water mixture.

Cook, stirring constantly, over medium heat until slightly thickened. Remove from the heat and cool. Beat the eggs with the sour cream until well blended. Stir in the raisin mixture and spoon into the pie shell.

Roll out the remaining dough ¼ inch thick and cut into ½-inch-wide strips. Using these strips, weave a latticework crust on top of the filling. Combine the tablespoon of water and egg yolk. Brush the top of the crust with the egg-water glaze and bake for 15 minutes. Reduce the heat to 350°F and bake for another 20 minutes, until well browned.

Yield: 10 to 12 servings

FARMHOUSE PUMPKIN PIE

Fall wouldn't be complete in the heartland without that old standby, pumpkin pie. This recipe is probably three times as old as I am but has remained virtually unchanged through the years.

1½ cups prepared pumpkin puree,
   canned or fresh (see Note)
⅓ cup granulated sugar
⅓ cup light brown sugar, packed
½ teaspoon salt
½ teaspoon ground ginger
¼ teaspoon ground nutmeg
Pinch ground clove
1 teaspoon ground cinnamon
Zest of 1 orange
3 eggs, beaten
¾ cup whole milk
¼ cup rum
1 cup heavy cream
1 10-inch prepared pie crust

Preheat the oven to 400°F. In a large mixing bowl combine the pumpkin puree, granulated sugar, brown sugar, salt, and spices. Fold in the orange zest and set aside.

Beat the eggs and add the milk, rum, and cream. Add this mixture to the reserved pumpkin mixture and blend well. Pour into the pie shell and bake for 10 minutes. Reduce the heat to 325°F and bake for an additional 30 to 40 minutes, until golden brown and firm to the touch.

Cool on a rack and serve with your favorite vanilla ice cream or with slightly sweetened whipped cream to which you have added a touch of rum.

Note: A 2¼-pound pumpkin makes 1½ cups puree. Preheat the oven to 350°F. Cut pumpkin in half and remove seeds. Place on a small cookie sheet and cover with foil. Bake on the center rack for 25 to 30 minutes until very soft. Remove and when cool enough to handle, scoop the flesh off the rind. Place in a food processor fitted with a steel blade and puree until smooth and velvety.

Yield: 10 to 12 servings

YAM-PECAN PIE

This combination of crunchy pecans in caramelized brown sugar and creamy, cinnamon-scented yam custard in a flaky crust has won rave reviews from our patrons. While sweet potatoes (which belong to the morning glory family) and yams are botanically different, they are interchangeable in this recipe.

1 10-inch prepared pie crust

PRALINE LAYER
4 tablespoons (1/2 stick) unsalted
   butter, melted
1 cup chopped pecans
1 cup light brown sugar, packed

CUSTARD
1¼ cups mashed, cooked yams
⅔ cup light brown sugar, packed
1 teaspoon ground ginger
1 teaspoon ground cinnamon
¼ teaspoon salt
1 cup half-and-half, scalded
3 eggs, beaten

TOPPING
4 tablespoons (1/2 stick) unsalted
   butter, softened
¾ cup light brown sugar, packed
3 cups chopped and whole pecans,
   combined

Prepare the pie crust and set aside. Preheat the oven to 375°F.

To make the praline layer, melt the butter and add the chopped pecans and the brown sugar. Bring to a boil until bubbling moderately. Remove from the heat and allow to cool. Spread evenly over the bottom of the prepared crust. Set aside.

Put all the ingredients for the custard in a bowl, in order, and mix thoroughly. Set aside.

To make the topping, blend the softened butter with the brown sugar and then stir in the pecans. Set aside.

Fill the reserved pie shell with the custard. Bake in the preheated oven for 20 to 25 minutes. Sprinkle the reserved topping evenly over the pie and bake for an additional 20 to 25 minutes, or until the custard is set and the crust is golden.

Yield: 10 to 12 servings

BLUE-RIBBON APPLE PIE

This recipe was developed for Prairie by Lois Levine. We think it's a blue-ribbon winner.

1 9-inch double pie crust
12 Granny Smith apples
⅔ cup dark brown sugar, packed
¼ cup granulated sugar
1½ teaspoons ground cinnamon
Juice of 1 lemon
1 tablespoon vanilla extract
½ teaspoon salt
⅓ cup all-purpose flour
4 tablespoons (½ stick) unsalted
    butter

STREUSEL
4½ tablespoons granulated sugar
¾ cup all-purpose flour
2 tablespoons unsalted butter
½ cup praline chips or Bits o'
    Brickle chips

EGG WASH
1 egg
2 tablespoons water

Preheat the oven to 350°F. Roll out the two crusts for the pie, and place the bottom crust in the pie plate. Prebake in the oven for 10 minutes. Set the other crust aside.

Peel, core, and slice the apples ¼ inch thick. Combine the brown sugar, granulated sugar, cinnamon, lemon juice, vanilla, salt, and flour. Toss the apple slices in the mixture.

In a large sauté pan, melt the butter and sauté the apple-sugar mixture in the pan until the apples are soft but not mushy. Remove and let cool.

Put the cooled apples in the prebaked pie crust. Combine the sugar, flour, and butter for the streusel. Mix well. Top the pie with the streusel and the praline chips. Combine the egg and water; mix well. Place the reserved top crust over all and crimp the edges to seal. Brush the top with the egg wash. Slash 4 or 5 openings in the crust for the steam to escape and put the pie in the preheated oven. Bake for 45 minutes. Remove and let cool for 30 minutes before serving.

Yield: 8 to 10 servings

BUTTERSCOTCH MERINGUE PIE

Smooth, gooey butterscotch is topped with an ultralight golden-brown meringue for this supersweet dessert.

1 9-inch prepared pie crust
⅓ cup all-purpose flour
1 cup light brown sugar, packed
¼ teaspoon salt
2 cups whole milk
3 egg yolks, beaten
3 tablespoons melted unsalted
   butter
1 cup prepared butterscotch
   topping
1 teaspoon vanilla extract

MERINGUE
6 egg whites
Pinch salt
½ teaspoon cream of tartar
½ cup granulated sugar

Preheat the oven to 350°F. Put about 2 cups of raw white rice in the pie crust. This will prevent air bubbles from forming in the crust as it bakes.

Bake the crust in the preheated oven on the center rack for 25 to 30 minutes. Remove and let cool. Reduce the heat to 325°F. Reserve the rice; you can use it again for baking pie shells.

In a large saucepan mix together the flour, brown sugar, and salt. Gradually stir in the milk, stirring constantly until well blended. Cook over medium heat for 15 minutes until well thickened, then cook 5 minutes longer, stirring only occasionally. Gradually pour a small amount of the hot milk mixture (about 1 cup) over the beaten egg yolks, stirring constantly so the egg yolks don't curdle. Slowly pour this egg mixture back into the milk mixture, stirring constantly. Put the pot back on the heat and cook over very low heat until good and thick. Add the butter, butterscotch topping, and vanilla and blend well.

Pour the filling into the prebaked pie shell and set aside. To prepare the meringue use a very clean, dry stainless-steel bowl. (You may want to wipe it out with white vinegar first, especially if it has been used recently for salad dressings.) In the bowl, sprinkle the salt and cream of tartar over the egg whites.

Whip on high speed to a coarse foam, and while the machine is still running, add the sugar very, very slowly. Continue to beat until stiff peaks appear. Pour the meringue over the filling, handling it extremely gently to avoid having the meringue lose volume. Cover all exposed butterscotch filling. Bake in the preheated oven on the center rack for about 25 minutes, or until the meringue is golden brown all over. Remove and let cool at least 2 hours before serving.

Yield: 8 to 10 servings

CARROT CAKE WITH ORANGE GLAZE

Departing a bit from tradition, this cake is served in a pool of orange glaze. The orange in the glaze brings out the flavor of the carrots, while at the same time the citric acid helps to cut through the richness of the cream-cheese frosting.

CAKE
2 cups all-purpose flour
2 teaspoons baking powder
1 teaspoon baking soda
1 teaspoon salt
½ teaspoon ground nutmeg
1 teaspoon ground cinnamon
1¼ cups peanut oil
1 cup dark brown sugar, packed
4 eggs
3 cups peeled, grated carrots
1 cup chopped pecans
1 teaspoon vanilla extract

CREAM CHEESE FROSTING
½ pound cream cheese, softened
8 tablespoons (1 stick) unsalted
   butter, softened
2 cups powdered sugar
1 tablespoon vanilla extract

ORANGE GLAZE
1 cup granulated sugar
1 cup frozen orange juice
   concentrate
1 teaspoon vanilla extract
1 cup sour cream

Preheat the oven to 350°F. Butter a 10-inch round cake pan. Set aside.

Sift together the flour, baking powder, baking soda, salt, nutmeg, and cinnamon. Set aside. In an electric mixer beat together the peanut oil and brown sugar. Add the reserved flour mixture and mix just until all ingredients are well blended.

Add the eggs, carrots, pecans, and vanilla. Mix well. Spoon the batter into the reserved cake pan. Place on the center rack of the preheated oven and bake for 90 minutes, or until toothpick inserted in the center comes out clean.

Remove from the oven and let cool. Remove the cake from the pan.

To make the frosting, combine the cream cheese and butter in a bowl. Using an electric mixer, beat on high speed until light and fluffy, about 8 to 10 minutes. Add the powdered sugar and vanilla and continue to beat another 5 minutes.

To make the glaze, combine the sugar, orange juice, and vanilla in a small saucepan. Bring to a boil and reduce the heat to a simmer. Simmer 10 to 12 minutes and remove from the heat. Let cool completely and then whisk in the sour cream.

Frost the top and sides of the cake. Serve with the Orange Glaze on the side.

Yield: 10 to 12 servings

OLD-FASHIONED PEACH GINGERBREAD UPSIDE-DOWN CAKE

Upside-down cakes are as much a part of culinary tradition in the Midwest as anywhere in America. Use only the ripest fresh peaches available and be sure to coat them well with the preserves so they won't dry out.

4 peaches, peeled, pitted, and
  sliced ¼ inch thick
1½ cups all-purpose flour
1½ teaspoons baking soda
⅓ cup molasses
¾ cup boiling water
2 eggs
¾ cup granulated sugar
⅓ cup unsalted butter, melted
8 peaches, peeled, pitted, and
  sliced ¼ inch thick
¼ cup melted unsalted butter
6 tablespoons dark brown sugar,
  packed
½ cup peach or apricot preserves

Preheat the oven to 350°F. Generously butter a 12-inch springform pan. Arrange the four sliced peaches in a circular pattern on the bottom of the pan. Set aside.

Sift together the flour and baking soda. Set aside. Combine the molasses and the water. Set aside. Combine the eggs and sugar in a mixing bowl and beat for 5 to 10 minutes, until light and fluffy. Add the melted butter gradually, while still beating.

Alternately add the reserved flour and molasses mixtures and mix just until smooth. Pour the batter over the peaches in the springform pan. Place on the center rack in the preheated oven and bake for about 45 minutes, or until toothpick inserted in the center comes out clean. Remove the cake from the oven and let cool.

Sauté the remaining peach slices in the 6 tablespoons of melted butter and the brown sugar, until soft but not mushy, about 6 to 8 minutes. Remove and let cool.

Invert the cake onto a serving platter so the peaches are on top. Arrange the cooled peach slices in a circular pattern around the top of the gingerbread cake. Melt the preserves in the top of a double boiler and generously brush over the sliced peaches.

Yield: 10 to 12 servings

SWEET POTATO-PRALINE CHEESECAKE

This thick, rich cheesecake is one that I invented in response to the great popularity of cheesecakes in Chicago. It combines pureed sweet potatoes with sugar, cinnamon, nutmeg, and mace, topped with an intense walnut praline. Be sure to take it out of the refrigerator an hour before serving, and because it is so rich, serve small slices.

CAKE
¾ cup sifted bread crumbs
¾ cup ground walnuts
8 tablespoons (1 stick) unsalted
    butter, melted
¼ cup powdered sugar
3 cups granulated sugar
1½ cups pureed cooked sweet
    potato (see Index)
10 egg yolks
3 tablespoons ground cinnamon
1 teaspoon ground mace
½ teaspoon ground nutmeg
1 teaspoon salt
3 pounds cream cheese
3 eggs
¼ cup heavy cream
2 tablespoons cornstarch
1 teaspoon vanilla extract

WALNUT PRALINE
1 cup toasted walnut pieces
    (see Note)
½ cup dark brown sugar, packed
¼ cup dark corn syrup

Preheat the oven to 450°F. Butter a 10-inch springform pan. In a food processor fitted with a metal blade or an electric mixer fitted with a paddle, blend together the bread crumbs, walnuts, butter, and powdered sugar.

Press this mixture into the buttered springform pan, spreading it evenly on the bottom and up the sides. Bake the crust on the center rack for 10 minutes. Remove and let cool.

In a large bowl combine half the granulated sugar with the pureed sweet potato, egg yolks, cinnamon, mace, nutmeg, and salt. Blend well and set aside.

In a food processor fitted with a metal blade or in the bowl of an electric mixer, cream together the cream cheese and the remaining sugar until very light and fluffy. Add the eggs, one at a time, beating well after each addition. Beat in the heavy cream, cornstarch, and vanilla. Gently fold in the reserved sweet-potato mixture. Pour the filling into the springform pan. Put the pan on the center rack of the preheated oven and bake for 10 minutes. Reduce the heat to 250°F and bake for 2 hours. Insert a toothpick in the center of the cake; when it comes out clean, the cake is done. Remove and let cool, leaving the cake in the pan.

Combine the ingredients for the praline in a small saucepan. Bring to a boil and reduce heat so that the mixture comes to a simmer. Simmer for 15 to 20 minutes, until thick, brown, and bubbly. Remove from the heat and remove from the pan immediately. Let cool 10 to 15 minutes before pouring over cheesecake. Chill cake 3 to 4 hours before serving.

Note: To toast walnuts, spread them on a cookie sheet and bake in a preheated 325°F oven for 5 to 8 minutes.

Yield: 8 to 10 servings

STEVE'S CHOCOLATE CAKE

My addiction to chocolate led me to invent this recipe. It is a two-layer cake consisting of a rich, dense, flourless chocolate-cake base topped with smooth, creamy, chocolate custard. Make the cake at least a day in advance so that the custard has time to set. Cut with a warm knife (run it under hot water) and serve with Dutch honey, which actually has no honey in it at all.

CAKE
1 pound semisweet chocolate
½ pound (2 sticks) unsalted butter
2 cups granulated sugar
¼ cup water
10 eggs, separated
1 ounce brandy

CHOCOLATE CREAM
2 cups granulated sugar
¾ cup water
¼ cup brandy
¾ pound semisweet chocolate
½ cup whole milk
2 tablespoons powdered gelatin
½ cup water
6 eggs, separated
1 quart heavy cream

DUTCH HONEY
1 cup granulated sugar
1 cup sour cream
1 cup dark corn syrup
1 teaspoon vanilla extract

Preheat the oven to 375°F. Butter a 10-inch springform pan well. Set aside.

Melt the chocolate and butter in the top of a double boiler over low heat.

In a large mixing bowl combine 1 cup of the sugar, water, egg yolks, and brandy. Using an electric mixer, beat on high speed until the mixture is light and fluffy. Using a rubber spatula, gently fold the chocolate mixture into the egg-yolk mixture. Set aside.

In another large bowl, using clean beaters, beat the egg whites on high speed to a coarse foam. While the machine is running, add the remaining sugar very, very slowly. Continue beating until stiff peaks appear.

Using a rubber spatula, gently fold the egg-white mixture into the reserved chocolate mixture. Pour the batter into the well-greased spring-form pan. Bake on the center rack for 20 minutes; lower the heat to 325°F and continue to bake for another 20 minutes. Remove and let cool, leaving the cake in the pan.

To make the chocolate cream, heat the sugar and water to boiling in a small saucepan. Reduce heat to a simmer and dissolve the sugar completely. Add the brandy. Set aside.

Combine the chocolate and milk in the top of a double boiler; melt the chocolate over low heat. Combine the gelatin with the ½ cup of water and let it set for 5 minutes. Heat until just warm in a microwave oven or in a small saucepan over a low flame. Add to the chocolate mixture.

Combine the chocolate mixture and the reserved sugar mixture. Beat the egg yolks, using an electric mixer, until light and fluffy. Using a rubber spatula, fold them gently into the chocolate mixture. Beat the egg whites until they hold stiff peaks and then fold them gently into the chocolate mixture. Beat the cream until stiff and gently fold into the chocolate mixture. Chill for 2 to 3 hours, until slightly thickened. Pour the chocolate cream over the cake and refrigerate overnight before serving.

To prepare the Dutch honey, combine all of the ingredients in a large stainless-steel bowl. Whisk well to dissolve the sugar. Serve in a pool with the cake.

Yield: 12 servings

WARM RHUBARB PIE
WITH STRAWBERRY-RHUBARB SAUCE

Use only fresh rhubarb in this recipe. (The season is fairly short, so take advantage of it while you can.)

CRUST
2 cups all-purpose flour
⅔ cup powdered sugar
1 cup (2 sticks) chilled butter, cut
   in chunks

FILLING
4 eggs
3 cups granulated sugar
½ cup all-purpose flour
1 teaspoon salt
2 tablespoons ground cinnamon
6 cups fresh rhubarb, cut into
   ¼-inch pieces

STRAWBERRY-RHUBARB
SAUCE
½ cup granulated sugar
½ cup water
1 cup finely sliced fresh rhubarb
1½ cups ripe strawberries, sliced

Preheat the oven to 350°F. Sift the flour and sugar together. Cut in the butter with a fork or pastry blender. Crust will resemble course meal. Pat into a 10-inch springform pan. Bake in the preheated oven for 15 minutes. Set aside.

    Mix the filling ingredients together in the order given. Pour into the prebaked crust and bake for 40 minutes, or until the filling is set. Let the pie rest for 20 to 30 minutes before serving.

To make the sauce, combine the sugar and the water in a saucepan and bring to a boil over medium heat. Stir constantly until all the sugar has dissolved.

Reduce the heat and add the rhubarb, cooking very slowly for about 25 minutes. The rhubarb should be soft and mushy. Add the strawberries and puree in a blender or food processor. Chill well. Serve the pie warm with the sauce.

Yield: 10 to 12 servings

PERSIMMON PUDDING WITH DRIED BLUEBERRIES

Persimmon pulp is available from Dymple's Delight, and dried blueberries from American Spoon Foods (see Sources for Midwest Specialties). What is neat about this recipe is that any type of squash or pumpkin may be substituted for persimmons, and any type of berry (dried, fresh, or frozen) may be substituted for the blueberries.

> 5 tablespoons unsalted butter
> 1 large persimmon
> 2 eggs
> ¾ cup dark brown sugar, packed
> ¾ cup all-purpose flour
> ½ teaspoon baking powder
> ½ teaspoon baking soda
> ¼ teaspoon salt
> 2 teaspoons ground cinnamon
> 1 teaspoon ground ginger
> ½ teaspoon ground nutmeg
> ¼ teaspoon ground clove
> 1 cup half-and-half
> ¼ cup dried blueberries
> 1 cup heavy cream (optional)
> Powdered sugar (optional)

Preheat the oven to 350°F. Using 1 tablespoon of the butter, grease the insides of eight ½-cup ramekins; set aside. Halve the persimmon lengthwise, scrape the flesh into the work bowl of a food processor fitted with a metal blade, and puree.

Measure 1 cup of the persimmon puree into a large bowl, discarding or reserving any remaining puree for another use. Mix the puree with the eggs and the brown sugar; set aside.

Sift the dry ingredients and spices together. Melt the remaining 4 tablespoons of butter and mix with the half-and-half. Stir the dry ingredients and the cream-butter mixture alternately into the reserved puree. Stir in the dried blueberries. Divide the mixture evenly between the buttered ramekins.

Adjust the oven rack to the middle setting and put the ramekins on a baking sheet. Put in the preheated oven and bake until the puddings are set and a knife inserted in the center comes out clean (30 to 35 minutes). Cool for 10 minutes. If desired, whip the cream until it forms soft peaks; top each pudding with a dollop of cream and sprinkle with powdered sugar.

Yield: 8 servings

WARM CHOCOLATE PUDDING CAKE WITH MARSHMALLOW-MINT WHIPPED CREAM

In this traditional dessert the top layer comes out like cake, the middle is dense chocolate, and the bottom becomes liquidy fudge. Top it with the light, refreshing Marshmallow-Mint Whipped Cream, mash it all together, and eat it with a spoon. It's a wonderful way to end any meal.

CAKE
1¼ cups granulated sugar
1 cup all-purpose flour
½ cup unsweetened cocoa
2 tablespoons baking powder
¼ teaspoon salt
½ cup whole milk
⅓ cup unsalted butter, melted
1½ teaspoons vanilla extract
½ cup dark brown sugar, packed
1½ cups boiling water

MARSHMALLOW-MINT WHIPPED CREAM
¾ cup mini marshmallows
¾ cup heavy cream
2 tablespoons mint extract
5 leaves fresh mint, chopped fine
Crème de menthe

Preheat the oven to 350°F. Butter 6 custard cups or ramekins. Set aside.

Combine ¾ cup of the sugar, flour, ¼ cup of the cocoa, baking powder, and salt. Mix well. Blend in the milk, butter, and vanilla. Pour ½ cup of the batter into each of the reserved custard cups or ramekins.

Combine the remaining sugar and cocoa with the brown sugar. Mix well. Sprinkle this mixture evenly over the batter in the cups. Top each with ¼ cup of the boiling water. Bake in the preheated oven on the center rack for 25 minutes or until firm.

To make the marshmallow cream, melt the marshmallows in the top of a double boiler over medium heat. Remove and set aside to cool. Whip the cream until stiff. Add the mint extract and chopped mint. Gently fold the melted marshmallows into the reserved whipped-cream mixture. Chill 2 to 3 hours before using.

Top each pudding with marshmallow mint cream and drizzle with crème de menthe. Serve warm!

Yield: 6 servings

BLACKBERRY COBBLER WITH MAPLE CUSTARD

To be truly authentic, serve this cobbler warm and top it at the last second with the smooth, velvety, maple custard, which should be made a day in advance.

PASTRY
2 teaspoons granulated sugar
1 cup all-purpose flour
1 tablespoon baking powder
½ teaspoon salt
4 tablespoons (½ stick) unsalted
    butter, softened
¼ cup heavy cream

BLACKBERRIES
3 cups fresh blackberries
¼ cup apple cider
¼ cup granulated sugar
2 tablespoons cornstarch
2 tablespoons heavy cream

MAPLE CUSTARD
1 teaspoon powdered gelatin
¼ cup water, at room temperature
¼ cup light brown sugar, packed
2 eggs, separated
Pinch salt
½ cup pure maple syrup
¼ cup granulated sugar
2 cups heavy cream

Preheat the oven to 400°F. Generously butter four 1-cup ramekins or one small (quart-sized) ovenproof casserole. Set aside.

To make the pastry, in a large bowl combine the sugar, flour, baking powder, and salt. Add the butter, and, using a fork or pastry blender, cut it into the flour mixture until it resembles coarse meal. Stir in the cream and mix quickly until the mixture forms a stiff dough that pulls away from the sides of the bowl.

On a floured board, using a floured rolling pin, roll out the dough to about ⅜ inch thick. Using a floured biscuit cutter, cut out 4 circles 2½ to 3 inches in diameter. Set the biscuits aside.

Wash and pick over the blackberries carefully; drain well. Combine the blackberries, apple cider, and sugar in a mixing bowl. Let stand and marinate for 1 to 2 hours.

Just before baking, remove about 2 tablespoons of the juice from the blackberries and mix it with the cornstarch. Add this back into the black-berry mixture. Divide the blackberries and their juices evenly among the ramekins (or place them in the casserole, laying the ramekins side by side) and top each ramekin with one precut biscuit. Brush the tops gently with the heavy cream and bake for 15 to 20 minutes, until the fruit is thick and bubbly and the crust is well browned. Let cool for 15 minutes before serving.

The custard should be refrigerated overnight before using. To make the custard, sprinkle the gelatin over the water and let it set for 5 minutes. Heat until just warm in a microwave oven or in a small saucepan over low heat. Set aside.

Place the brown sugar, egg yolks, and salt in the bowl of an electric mixer and beat for 5 to 10 minutes, until very light and fluffy. Add the reserved gelatin mixture and mix well. Stir in the maple syrup and set aside. Whip the egg whites until they form a coarse foam. Add the sugar very, very slowly and continue to beat until the egg whites reach the medium-peak stage. Whip the cream until stiff and set aside. Using a rubber spatula, gently fold the egg whites into the reserved egg-yolk mixture. Gently fold in the reserved whipped cream. Serve each cobbler topped with maple custard.

Yield: 4 servings

WALNUT AND CARAMEL SCHAUM TORTES

Schaum torte is popular in the Milwaukee area and typically consists of a simple meringue topped with strawberries and whipped cream. My recipe is a sort of deluxe version.

Softened unsalted butter
Granulated sugar
¾ cup chopped, toasted walnuts
   (see Note 1)
½ cup dried bread crumbs
1 teaspoon baking powder
3 egg whites
¾ cup granulated sugar

CARAMEL SAUCE (see Note 2)
1 cup granulated sugar
2½ cups cold water
Juice of 1 lemon

INGREDIENTS FOR
ASSEMBLY
Vanilla ice cream
2 cups whipped cream
48 to 50 strawberries, washed,
   hulled, and quartered
Powdered sugar
16 tablespoons chopped, toasted
   walnuts
Mint leaves (optional)

Preheat the oven to 375°F. Brush the insides of 8 muffin cups with butter. (It's best to use a nonstick, coated muffin pan.) Sprinkle with sugar, invert, and tap the pan to remove excess sugar. Set aside.

To make the tortes, mix the walnuts, bread crumbs, and baking powder in a bowl; set aside. In a separate bowl, beat the egg whites until stiff but not dry, adding sugar gradually and beating well after each addition. Fold the nut mixture very gently into the egg whites, using a rubber spatula. Spoon the meringue into the prepared muffin tins, dividing it evenly. Bake in the preheated oven for 45 minutes to 1 hour, until lightly brown and dry

to the touch. Remove from the oven and let the tortes cool in the pan. Gently remove them from the pans and set aside.

To make the caramel sauce, place the sugar and 1 cup of the water in a heavy-bottomed saucepan and bring the mixture to a full boil over medium heat. Make sure there are no sugar granules clinging to the sides of the pan. To avoid this, keep a small bowl of water and a pastry brush on the side, and brush down the sides of the pan as needed to avoid crystallization.

Cook the syrup over medium heat until it reduces and begins to brown (the "caramel stage" on your candy thermometer). You want a nice, deep, amber color, almost to the point of burning. When the syrup reaches this stage, you must *immediately* add the remaining 1½ cups of cold water. *This is potentially dangerous.* You can burn yourself badly if you're not careful. Remove the pan from the burner and place it a good arm's length away. Pour in the water all at once, but carefully, because it is apt to splatter and boil up.

If you've done it correctly, the result will be a hard, gooey mass of brown sugar. Add the lemon juice. Return the pan to low heat and melt this mass back into a liquid. Strain it through a fine mesh cap or sieve. Let cool to room temperature and reserve.

To assemble: Split each torte in half and place the bottom half on a serving dish. Place a scoop of the vanilla ice cream on top. Top with 1 tablespoon of whipped cream, and add the remaining torte half. Arrange 6 to 8 hulled and quartered strawberries around the torte. Top with another tablespoon of whipped cream, a good sprinkling of powdered sugar, and 2 tablespoons of the chopped, toasted walnuts. Top with 1 to 2 tablespoons of the caramel sauce, and garnish with the mint leaves, if desired.

Note 1: To toast walnuts, spread them out on a cookie sheet and bake in a preheated 325°F oven for 5 to 8 minutes.
Note 2: A candy thermometer is essential for making the caramel in this recipe. For safety reasons, read the recipe all the way through, and follow the directions explicitly. Make sure that you are fully clothed—no shorts or bare midriff. Wear an apron and have oven mitts handy.

Yield: 8 servings

TRADITIONAL BLUEBERRY SHORTCAKE

You may substitute other berries for the blueberries in this recipe.

SHORTCAKE
3 cups all-purpose flour
$\frac{1}{3}$ cup granulated sugar
2 tablespoons baking powder
1 tablespoon salt
$\frac{3}{4}$ cup (sticks) unsalted butter, cut
    into $\frac{1}{2}$-inch cubes
1 cup heavy cream
$\frac{1}{4}$ cup ($\frac{1}{2}$ stick) melted unsalted
    butter
$\frac{1}{4}$ cup heavy cream
4 tablespoons granulated sugar

BLUEBERRY COMPOTE
6 cups fresh blueberries
$\frac{2}{3}$ cup granulated sugar
Juice of $\frac{1}{2}$ lemon

ASSEMBLY FOR EACH
PORTION
4 shortcakes
1 large scoop premium vanilla ice
    cream
$\frac{3}{4}$ cup whipped cream (6 cups
    total)
$\frac{1}{2}$ to $\frac{3}{4}$ cup Blueberry Compote
Powdered sugar

Preheat the oven to 400°F. Cover a cookie sheet with parchment paper. Sift together the flour, sugar, baking powder, and salt. Add the butter and gently mix with a fork or pastry blender until the mixture resembles coarse meal. Stir in enough cream so that the pastry just holds together to form a soft dough.

Gently roll out the dough on a floured surface to ¼ inch thick. Brush the dough generously with the melted butter and fold it in half to form a double layer. Cut into 3-inch rounds using a floured cookie cutter. Arrange on the cookie sheet and bake in the preheated oven for 15 minutes, until the shortcakes are puffed and golden brown. About 2 minutes prior to removing the shortcakes from the oven, brush with heavy cream and sprinkle with sugar. Remove and set aside.

While the shortcakes bake, pick over the berries and wash them in cold water. Place 3 cups of the berries in a medium saucepan and add the sugar and lemon juice. Cook the berries, covered, over low heat for 10 minutes. Remove the cover and cook over high heat until the juices thicken. Remove from the heat and let cool. Stir in the remaining 3 cups of berries.

To assemble each portion, place one shortcake in the center of a large plate. Top with ice cream; add whipped cream. Carefully spoon the Blueberry Compote over the top. Place the remaining 3 shortcakes around the top; sprinkle with powdered sugar. Serve immediately.

Yield: 8 servings

MENUS

Recipes marked with an asterisk (*) are included in this book.

A DINNER FOR THE CHAINE DES ROTISSEURS

In preparing the menu for this black-tie dinner, we tried to combine items that were traditionally midwestern with a more formal French setting. The consommé was served in hollowed-out miniature pumpkins, and we made our own version of apple brandy by adding apple cider, clove, and cinnamon to some Calvados. It turned out great!

Smoked Trout Mousse on Spoons with Hackleback Sturgeon Caviar
1985 Scharffenberger Brut, Blanc de Blancs, Mendocino

Fillet of Coho Salmon Stuffed with Forest Mushrooms
1985 Château St. Belle Terre Vineyard Chardonnay, Sonoma

Smoked Turkey Consommé with Pumpkin Dumplings,
Peas, and Duck Liver

Grilled Fillet of Michigan Buffalo with Regional Autumn Vegetables
1985 Adelsheim Pinot Noir, Willamette Valley

Medley of Wisconsin Farmstead Cheeses

Individual Apple-Quince Crumble with Maple Custard Sauce
Prairie Apple Brandy

THANKSGIVING DAY DINNER

What is more traditional in the heartland than Thanksgiving dinner with all the trimmings? Thanksgiving is truly an American feast, handed down from our forefathers. They borrowed the tradition from the Indians who gave thanks to their gods for a good harvest season of squash, pumpkins, maize, beans, and berries.

It's interesting to note that the turkey was first domesticated by the Aztecs and that the wild turkey is native to North America.

*Buckwheat Honey Bread

*Warm Apple and Sage Sausage Turnovers with Cider-Cranberry Glaze

*Sweet-and-Tart Pickled Cranberries
Root-Vegetable Relish Mix

*Traditional Roast Turkey with Whole-Wheat Sage Stuffing and
Giblet Gravy

*Glazed Turnips
*Wild Rice and Mushroom Casserole
*Dilled Baby Carrots

*Yam-Pecan Pie
*Farmhouse Pumpkin Pie

NEW YEAR'S EVE DINNER

This was our very first New Year's Eve dinner. Although I don't know where it started, it's traditional to serve game on New Year's Eve. The carrot soup can be made using the recipe for Simple Cream of Asparagus Soup and substituting carrots for the asparagus.

*Smoked Trout Terrine with Horseradish-Dill Mayonnaise

Cream of Carrot Soup with Apple Butter and Freshly Grated Nutmeg

Medley of Field Greens with Smoked Wisconsin Duck Breast

*Pepper-Crusted Venison Steak in a Blackberry Glaze
Glazed Celery Root
Sweet-Potato Straws

*Walnut and Caramel Schaum Tortes

FEBRUARY DINNER

It can get pretty damn cold in the Midwest during the winter. A warm stew is perfect for one of those cold winter days. The burgoo is made with buffalo, which is much healthier than beef, as it is lower in cholesterol and higher in protein.

*Mustard Pickles
*Wisconsin Cheddar Cheese and Chive Drop Biscuits

*Corn Chowder with Fresh Herbs and Country-Smoked Ham

*Grilled Duck Breast Salad with Honey-Thyme Vinegar and
Pickled Cranberries

*Prairie Buffalo Burgoo, Rabbit Sausage, and Root-Vegetable Relish Mix
*Broccoli Fritters with Cheddar Hollandaise

*Warm Chocolate Pudding Cake with Marshmallow-Mint
Whipped Cream

THE RESTAURANT SHOW MENU

Every year the National Restaurant Association holds its annual convention right here in Chicago. For us, it's a chance to show the people in our business the great products and traditions we have in the Midwest. This is a tasting menu we created for the show in 1989.

Thinly Sliced Applewood-Smoked Catfish with Red-Onion Relish

Alphabet Soup with Turkey, Baby Corn, and Fiddleheads

Medley of Spring Greens with Country Ham and Blue Cheese

Three Little Quails in Rosemary-Infused Giblet Gravy
or
Grilled Spring Chicken in Natural Juices with Michigan Morels
or
Baked Farm-Raised Brook Trout with Lemon, Sour Cream, and Herbs

Gingered Caramel-Crusted Berry Custard with Wildflower Honey

LIGHT SPRING LUNCH

This menu consists of some of our bestselling dishes on the spring menu, which rolls out about mid-May when morels, ramps, asparagus, and rhubarb come into season.

*Carrot-Raisin-Bran Muffins

*Simple Cream of Asparagus Soup

*Fried Chicken and Baby Lettuce Salad

*Warm Rhubarb Crisp with Strawberry-Rhubarb Sauce

FOURTH OF JULY PICNIC

Prepare the Honey-Mustard Sauce ahead of time and grill the chicken while basting it with the sauce. Relishes and condiments are perfect for picnics.

*Buckwheat Honey Bread

*Chilled Ham-Pear Loaf with Three-Berry Relish

*Cucumber Relish
*Amish Potato Salad
*Pear-Honey Chutney

*Grilled Honey-Mustard Chicken
*Barbecued Corn on the Cob

*Dairyland Sour Cream–Raisin Pie

APPLE FEST

Every year during the fall we have an Apple Fest at Prairie. The goal is to make as many different dishes with apples as possible. It's amazing how many varieties of apples there are.

*Cider-Squash Bread

*Warm Spinach Salad with Sliced Pork Loin and Apple-Caraway Kraut

*Stuffed Shoulder of Veal with Apples, Chestnuts, and Cranberries
*Celery Root Puree

*Blue-Ribbon Apple Pie

MIDWESTERN DINNER WITH FRENCH WINES

This is another interesting dinner we created, pairing French wines with midwestern food. The sauternes went especially well with the Persimmon Pudding.

*Savory Bread Pudding with Smoked Duck
Three-Vegetable Puree
Hermitage Blanc, 1980
E. Guigal
Côtes du Rhône

Roasted Loin of Provimi Veal with Apples, Chestnuts, and Cranberries
Glazed Acorn Squash
*Pearl Barley Pilaf
Beaune, 1978
Côte de Beaune
May Quenot
Burgundy

An assortment of Wisconsin Cheeses
Millet–Whole-Wheat Bread

*Persimmon Pudding with Dried Blueberries
Château Climens, 1975
Barsac
Sauternes

SOURCES FOR MIDWEST SPECIALTIES

Alyce's Herbs
P.O. Box 9563
Madison, Wisconsin 53715
(608) 274-4911
Herb vinegars; herbs; unusual
produce; edible flowers

American Spoon Foods, Inc.
411 East Lake Street
Petoskey, Michigan 49770
1 (800) 222-5886
Dried cherries and blueberries;
spoon fruits and butters, fruit
preserves, jellies, and marmalades;
honey; maple syrup; Genovese
sun-dried tomatoes from Ohio;
Missouri pecans; midwestern
whitefish caviar; morels

Applesource
Route 1
Chapin, Illinois 62628
(217) 245-7589
Hundreds of varieties of apples

Brumwell Flour Mill
South Amana, Iowa 52334
(319) 622-3455
Flours; cornmeal; rye meal and
flour; pancake and waffle mixes;
cookie mix; cornbread mix

Bruss Meat Company
3548 North Kostner
Chicago, Illinois 60641
(312) 282-2900
Certified Angus beef; veal; lamb;
pork; poultry; game, including
buffalo and free-range hens

Cavanaugh Lakeview Farms, Ltd.
P.O. Box 580
Chelsea, Michigan 48118-0430
1 (800) 243-4438
Honey-cured smoked poultry;
ham; duck; other meats

Collins Caviar
6210 Robin Lane
Crystal Lake, Illinois 60014
(815) 459-6210
Midwestern caviar, fish products,
and sturgeon

Country Connection
1704 Central Street
Evanston, Illinois 60201
(708) 256-1968
Complete assortment of
wonderful, handmade farmstead
cheeses from southwestern
Wisconsin

Dandy Pantry
212 Hammonds Drive East
Stockton, Missouri 65785
1 (800) 872-6879
American black walnuts, pecans,
and hickory nuts

Dymple's Delight
Route 4, Box 53
Mitchell, Indiana 47446
(812) 849-3487
Fresh and canned persimmons

Fantome Farms
Rural Route 1, Box 158
Ridgeway, Wisconsin 53582
(608) 924-1266
Goat cheeses

Green River Trout Farm
Route 1, Box 267
Mancelona, Michigan 49659
(616) 584-3486
Farm-raised trout; hickory-smoked
trout; pheasant; game hen; quail;
duck and capons; fresh morels;
Michigan leeks; venison; buffalo;
Michigan snapper turtle

Herb Gathering, Inc.
5742 Kenwood Avenue
Kansas City, Missouri 64110
(816) 523-2653
Fresh herbs and edible flowers

Maple Leaf Farms
P.O. Box 308
Milford, Indiana 46542-0308
(219) 658-2208
Ducks

Maytag Dairy Farms
Rural Route 1, Box 806
Newton, Iowa 50208
(515) 792-1133
Maytag blue cheese

Michigan Asparagus Board
P.O. Box 23218
Lansing, Michigan 48909
(515) 323-7000
Michigan asparagus

Nauvoo Blue Cheese Company
1095 Young Street
Nauvoo, Illinois 62354
(217) 453-2213
Nauvoo blue cheese

Nueske Hillcrest Farm Meats
Rural Route 2
Wittenberg, Wisconsin 54499
(715) 253-2226
Applewood-smoked sausage,
hams, bacons, kielbasa, bratwurst,
duck, turkey, chicken, and pork
chops

Prairie Farm Specialties
Route 1, Box 301
Waterman, Illinois 60556
(815) 758-6859
Free-range chicken; pheasant

Reutenik Gardens
826 East Schaff Road
Brooklin Heights, Ohio 44131
(216) 741-1443
Fresh herbs

Reynolds Sugar Bush
Aniwa, Wisconsin 54408
(715) 449-2057 *or* 2536
Maple syrup; maple products;
fruit syrups

Rothschild Berry Farm, Inc.
Urbana, Ohio 43078
1 (800) 356-7397
Mustards; preserves; vinegars;
berry products

Voyageur Trading Company
P.O. Box 35121
Minneapolis, Minnesota 55435
1 (800) 445-7643
Wild rice

Wild Game, Inc.
2315 West Huron
Chicago, Illinois 60612
(312) 278-1661
Big game, including venison,
buffalo, and antelope; small game,
including rabbit and hare; game
birds, including duck, pheasant,
quail, and partridge; smoked fish
and specialty items, including
American cheeses such as Maytag
blue and Illinois brie; wild
berries; buffalo, venison, and
rabbit sausages

MIDWESTERN FOOD FESTIVALS

MAY

Cadillac Mushroom Festival
Cadillac, Michigan
(616) 775-9776

Harrison Mushroom Festival
Harrison, Michigan
(517) 539-6011

Maple Festival
Reynolds Sugar Bush
Aniwa, Wisconsin
(715) 449-2057
Last Sunday in May

Morel Mushroom Festival
Lewiston, Michigan
(517) 786-2293

Morel Mushroom Festival
Muscoda, Wisconsin
(608) 739-3639

Mushroom Festival
Mesick, Michigan
(616) 885-1370

Mushroom Hunting
Mansfield, Indiana
(317) 653-3141

National Mushroom Hunting
Championship
Boyne City, Michigan
(616) 582-6222
Mother's Day weekend

JUNE

National Asparagus Festival
Box 153
Shelby/Hart, Michigan
Second weekend in June

JULY

Cheese Days
Colby, Wisconsin
(715) 223-4410

Minnesota Wild Rice Festival
Keliher, Washkish, Minnesota
Early in the month

National Cherry Festival
P.O. Box 141
Traverse City, Michigan
Early in the month

AUGUST

Sweet Corn Festival
Sun Prairie, Wisconsin
(608) 837-4547
Mid-August weekend

SEPTEMBER

Blair Annual Cheese Festival
Blair, Wisconsin
(608) 989-2542
Second weekend in September

Persimmon Festival
Mitchell, Indiana
(812) 849-2151
Last week of the month

OCTOBER

Bayfield Apple Festival
Bayfield, Wisconsin
(715) 779-3335
First weekend in month

Cranberry Festival
Eagle River, Wisconsin
(715) 449-2057
First weekend in month

INDEX

197